I0425951

February 2012

Follow-up on 2011 Report: Status of Actions Taken to Reduce Duplication, Overlap, and Fragmentation, Save Tax Dollars, and Enhance Revenue

Contents

Abbreviations

ASC	alternative simplified credit
ATF	Bureau of Alcohol, Tobacco, Firearms, and Explosives
BEST	Border Enforcement Security Task Force
BLM	Bureau of Land Management
CBP	Customs and Border Protection
CDE	Community Development Entity
CIO	Chief Information Officer
CMS	Centers for Medicare & Medicaid Services
Commerce	Department of Commerce
CDBG	Community Development Block Grant
Coordinating Council	Interagency Transportation Coordinating Council on Access and Mobility
Corps	U.S. Army Corps of Engineers
CPRA	Civilian Real Property Realignment Act
DHS	Department of Homeland Security
DOD	Department of Defense
DOT	Department of Transportation
EAS	Essential Air Service
EDA	Economic Development Administration
ESEA	Elementary and Secondary Education Act of 1965
FAM	Foreign Affairs Manual
FBI	Federal Bureau of Investigation
FCC	Federal Communications Commission
FEMA	Federal Emergency Management Agency
FMCSA	Federal Motor Carrier Safety Administration
GPRAMA	Government Performance and Results Modernization Act of 2010
GSA	General Services Administration
HHS	Department of Health and Human Services
HUD	Department of Housing and Urban Development
IBET	Integrated Border Enforcement Team
IED	improvised explosive device
iEHR	integrated electronic health record
IILCM	integrated investment life cycle model
Interior	Department of the Interior
IPERA	Improper Payments Elimination and Recovery Act of 2010
IRS	Internal Revenue Service
IT	information technology
JIEDDO	Joint Improvised Explosive Device Defeat Organization
Justice	Department of Justice

Labor	Department of Labor
MOU	memorandum of understanding
MPPR	multiple procedure payment reduction
NSS	National Security Staff
OFPP	Office of Federal Procurement Policy
OMB	Office of Management and Budget
O&S	operating and support
PAR	Performance and Accountability Report
RAC	recovery audit contractor
R&D	research and development
ROI	return on investment
SBA	Small Business Administration
SIOC	Strategic Information Operation Centers
SPOT	Screening of Passengers by Observation Techniques
S&T	Science and Technology Directorate
State	Department of State
TANF	Temporary Assistance for Needy Families
T&E	testing and evaluation
Treasury	Department of the Treasury
TRIAD	Transit and Rail Intelligence Awareness Daily
TSA	Transportation Security Administration
USAID	U.S. Agency for International Development
USDA	U.S. Department of Agriculture
USICH	U.S. Interagency Council on Homelessness
VA	Department of Veterans Affairs
VEETC	Volumetric Ethanol Excise Tax Credit
VR	vocational rehabilitation

United States Government Accountability Office
Washington, DC 20548

February 28, 2012

Congressional Addressees

In March 2011, GAO issued its first annual report to the Congress on potential duplication, overlap, and fragmentation in the federal government.[1] The report also identified opportunities to achieve cost savings and enhance revenues. We identified 81 areas—which span a wide range of government missions[2]—with a total of 176 actions[3] that the Congress and the executive branch could take to reduce or eliminate unnecessary duplication, overlap, and fragmentation or achieve other potential financial benefits. We also presented areas where programs may be able to achieve greater efficiencies or become more effective in providing government services. In many areas, we suggested actions— identifying some new options, as well as underscoring numerous existing GAO recommendations—that policymakers could consider. This status report provides an overall assessment of progress in implementing actions for the 81 areas, as well as an assessment of each of the 176 suggested actions.

As of February 10, 2012, the Congress and the executive branch had made some progress in addressing the majority of the 81 areas that we identified, including the implementation of all actions in 4 areas; however, additional steps are needed to fully implement the remaining actions to achieve associated benefits. GAO suggested a wide range of actions for the Congress and the executive branch to consider, such as developing strategies to better coordinate fragmented efforts, implementing executive

---

[1]GAO, *Opportunities to Reduce Potential Duplication in Government Programs, Save Tax Dollars, and Enhance Revenue*, GAO-11-318SP (Washington, D.C.: Mar. 1, 2011). This report was issued in response to a new statutory requirement that GAO identify federal programs, agencies, offices, and initiatives, either within departments or governmentwide, which have duplicative goals or activities. Congress asked GAO to conduct this work and to report annually on our findings. See Pub. L. No. 111-139, §21, 124 Stat. 29 (2010), 31 U.S.C. § 712 Note.

[2]Agriculture, defense, economic development, energy, general government, health, homeland security, international affairs, and social services were among the government missions included in the March 2011 report.

[3]These actions were identified in the "Actions Needed" section for each respective issue area.

initiatives to improve oversight and evaluation of overlapping programs, considering enactment of legislation to facilitate revenue collection, and examining opportunities to eliminate potential duplication through streamlining, collocating, or consolidating program efforts or administrative services.

GAO's specific assessment of progress as of February 10, 2012, showed that 4 (or 5 percent) of the 81 areas GAO identified were addressed; 60 (or 74 percent) were partially addressed; and 17 (or 21 percent) were not addressed. Enclosure I presents GAO's assessment of the overall progress made in each area. GAO applied the following criteria in making these overall assessments for the 81 areas. We determined that an area was:

- "addressed" if all actions needed in that area were addressed;

- "partially addressed" if at least one action needed in that area showed some progress toward implementation, but not all actions were addressed; and

- "not addressed" if none of the actions needed in that area were addressed.

As of February 10, 2012, the majority of 176 actions needed within the 81 areas identified by GAO have been partially addressed. Specifically, 23 (or 13 percent) were addressed[4]; 99 (or 56 percent) were partially addressed; 54 (or 31 percent) were not addressed[5]. Enclosure II presents a progress update for each of the 176 legislative and executive actions needed that GAO identified within the 81 areas, as well as GAO's assessment of that progress. GAO applied the following criteria in making these assessments.

---

[4]In one instance, the legislative action needed required Congress to consider several options, including allowing a tax credit to expire. Thus, because Congress did not renew the provision, the action was considered addressed.

[5]Members of Congress have introduced a wide range of bills and amendments, that if enacted, could help address a number of the issues raised in our March 2011 report. However, for the purposes of this report, only those bills that have passed a committee are discussed in the progress updates contained in Enclosure II.

For legislative branch actions:

- "addressed," means relevant legislation is enacted and addresses all aspects of the action needed;[6]

- "partially addressed," means a relevant bill has passed a committee, the House or Senate, or relevant legislation has been enacted, but only addressed part of the action needed; and

- "not addressed," means a bill may have been introduced, but did not pass out of a committee, or no relevant legislation has been introduced.

For executive branch actions:

- "addressed," means implementation of the action needed has been completed;

- "partially addressed," means the action needed is in development, started but not yet completed;

- "not addressed," means the administration and/or agencies have made minimal or no progress toward implementing the action needed.

In addition to the actions taken reported above, Congress has held a number of hearings and the Office of Management and Budget (OMB) has provided guidance to executive branch agencies on areas that GAO identified that could benefit from increased attention and ongoing oversight. Since the issuance of our March 2011 report, GAO has testified numerous times on its first annual report and on specific issues highlighted in the report. On August 17, 2011, OMB issued its Fiscal Year 2013 Budget Guidance, which stated that agencies' 2013 budget submissions and management plans should take into consideration areas of duplication or overlap identified by GAO, as well as by others. The guidance also advised agencies to take a number of other steps to achieve efficiency increases, such as identifying and including in their

---

[6]In situations where our action needed suggested that Congress should let a provision expire, we classified it as "addressed" if Congress permitted such expiration to happen.

budget submissions cost-saving efforts that will improve operational efficiency and taxpayers' rate of return, including program integration, reorganizations within and between agency components, and resource realignment to improve public services.

Streamlining federal efforts, reducing government costs, and enhancing revenue collections can offer financial and other benefits. Today, and concurrently with this report, GAO issued its second annual report to Congress in response to the statutory requirement that GAO identify federal programs, agencies, offices, and initiatives with duplicative goals or activities.[7] That report identifies 51 additional issue areas and numerous actions within those issue areas that, if implemented, may further improve programs' effectiveness and efficiency, achieve cost savings, and enhance revenues.

Opportunities exist for the Congress and federal agencies to continue to address the identified actions needed in our March 2011 and February 2012 reports. Collectively, these reports show that, if the actions are implemented, the government could save tens of billions of dollars annually. A number of the issues are difficult to address and implementing many of the actions identified will take time and sustained leadership.

To prepare this report, we conducted our work from July 2011 through February 2012 in accordance with all sections of GAO's Quality Assurance Framework that are relevant to our objectives. The framework requires that we plan and perform the engagement to meet our stated objectives and to discuss any limitations in our work. We believe that the information and data obtained, and the analysis conducted, provide a reasonable basis for any findings and conclusions in this product. GAO provided the draft to the agencies involved and OMB for their comments and incorporated comments as appropriate. The information in this report is current as of February 10, 2012 and does not reflect any actions that might have been taken after that date. Enclosure III contains additional details of our scope and methodology.

---

[7]GAO, *2012 Annual Report: Opportunities to Reduce Duplication, Overlap and Fragmentation, Achieve Savings, and Enhance Revenue,* GAO-12-342SP (Washington, D.C.: February 28, 2012).

This report was prepared under the coordination of Janet St. Laurent, Managing Director, Defense Capabilities and Management, who may be reached at (202) 512-4300, or stlaurentj@gao.gov and Zina Merritt, Director, Defense Capabilities and Management, who may be reached at (202) 512-4300 or merrittz@gao.gov.

Gene L. Dodaro
Comptroller General
   of the United States

List of Congressional Addressees

The Honorable Daniel K. Inouye
Chairman
The Honorable Thad Cochran
Vice Chairman
Committee on Appropriations
United States Senate

The Honorable Kent Conrad
Chairman
The Honorable Jeff Sessions
Ranking Member
Committee on the Budget
United States Senate

The Honorable Joseph I. Lieberman
Chairman
The Honorable Susan M. Collins
Ranking Member
Committee on Homeland Security
   and Governmental Affairs
United States Senate

The Honorable Harold Rogers
Chairman
The Honorable Norman D. Dicks
Ranking Member
Committee on Appropriations
House of Representatives

The Honorable Paul Ryan
Chairman
The Honorable Chris Van Hollen
Ranking Member
Committee on the Budget
House of Representatives

The Honorable Darrell Issa
Chairman
The Honorable Elijah E. Cummings
Ranking Member
Committee on Oversight
   and Government Reform
House of Representatives

The Honorable Scott Brown
United States Senate

The Honorable Tom Coburn
United States Senate

The Honorable Claire McCaskill
United States Senate

The Honorable Mark R. Warner
United States Senate

Enclosure I: Overall Progress Made in Each of the 81 Areas

This enclosure presents a summary of GAO's assessment of the overall progress made in each of the 81 areas that we identified in our March 2011 report[1] in which the Congress and the executive branch could take actions to reduce or eliminate potential duplication, overlap, and fragmentation or achieve other potential financial benefits. For each of the 34 areas related to duplication, overlap, or fragmentation that GAO identified, table 1 presents GAO's assessment of the overall progress made in implementing the actions needed in that area. For each of the 47 areas where GAO identified cost saving or revenue enhancement opportunities, table 2 presents GAO's assessment of the overall progress made in implementing the actions GAO identified.

Table 1: Overall Progress Made in Each of the GAO Identified Areas of Potential Duplication, Overlap, and Fragmentation, as of February 10, 2012

Mission	Areas identified		Assessment	Page
Agriculture	1.	Fragmented **food safety** system has caused inconsistent oversight, ineffective coordination, and inefficient use of resources	◐	14
Defense	2.	Realigning **DOD's military medical command** structures and consolidating common functions could increase efficiency and result in projected savings ranging from $281 million to $460 million annually	◐	15
	3.	Opportunities exist for consolidation and increased efficiencies to maximize response to **warfighter urgent needs**	◐	16
	4.	Opportunities exist to avoid unnecessary redundancies and improve the coordination of **counter-improvised explosive device efforts**	◐	17
	5.	Opportunities exist to avoid unnecessary redundancies and maximize the efficient use of **intelligence, surveillance,** and **reconnaissance** capabilities	◐	18
	6.	A departmentwide acquisition strategy could reduce DOD's risk of costly duplication in purchasing **Tactical Wheeled Vehicles**	◐	19
	7.	Improved joint oversight of DOD's **prepositioning programs** for equipment and supplies may reduce unnecessary duplication	◐	20
	8.	**DOD's business systems** modernization: opportunities exist for optimizing business operations and systems	◐	21

[1]GAO, *Opportunities to Reduce Potential Duplication in Government Programs, Save Tax Dollars, and Enhance Revenue,* GAO-11-318SP (Washington, D.C.: Mar. 1, 2011).

Mission	Areas identified	Assessment	Page
Economic development	9. The efficiency and effectiveness of fragmented **economic development programs** are unclear	◑	23
	10. The federal approach to **surface transportation** is fragmented, lacks clear goals, and is not accountable for results	◑	25
	11. Fragmented federal efforts to meet **water needs** in the **U.S.-Mexico border region** have resulted in an administrative burden, redundant activities, and an overall inefficient use of resources	○	26
Energy	12. Resolving conflicting requirements could more effectively achieve **federal fleet energy goals**	○	27
	13. Addressing duplicative federal efforts directed at increasing **domestic ethanol production** could reduce revenue losses by more than $5.7 billion annually	●	28
General government	14. **Enterprise architectures:** key mechanisms for identifying potential overlap and duplication	◑	29
	15. Consolidating **federal data** centers provides opportunity to improve government efficiency	◑	30
	16. Collecting improved data on **interagency contracting** to minimize duplication could help the government leverage its vast buying power	◑	31
	17. Periodic reviews could help identify ineffective **tax expenditures** and redundancies in related tax and spending programs, potentially reducing revenue losses by billions of dollars	○	32
Health	18. Opportunities exist for **DOD** and **VA** to jointly modernize their **electronic health record systems**	◑	34
	19. **VA** and **DOD** need to control **drug** costs and increase **joint contracting** wherever it is cost-effective	◑	35
	20. HHS needs an overall strategy to better integrate nationwide **public health information** systems	○	37
Homeland security/ Law enforcement	21. Strategic oversight mechanisms could help integrate fragmented interagency efforts to defend against **biological threats**	◑	38
	22. DHS oversight could help eliminate potential duplicating efforts of interagency forums in **securing** the **northern border**	○	39
	23. The Department of Justice plans actions to reduce overlap in **explosives investigations**, but monitoring is needed to ensure successful implementation	●	40
	24. **TSA's security assessments** on commercial trucking companies overlap with those of another agency, but efforts are under way to address the overlap	◑	41
	25. DHS could streamline mechanisms for **sharing security-related information** with **public transit agencies** to help address overlapping information	◑	42
	26. **FEMA** needs to improve its oversight of **grants** and establish a framework for assessing capabilities to identify gaps and prioritize investments	◑	43

Mission	Areas identified	Assessment	Page
International affairs	27. Lack of information sharing could create the potential for duplication of efforts between U.S. agencies involved in **development efforts** in **Afghanistan**	◑	46
	28. Despite restructuring, overlapping roles and functions still exist at State's **Arms Control** and **Nonproliferation Bureaus**	●	47
Social services	29. Actions needed to reduce administrative overlap among **domestic food assistance** programs	○	48
	30. Better coordination of federal **homelessness** programs may minimize fragmentation and overlap	◑	49
	31. Further steps needed to improve cost-effectiveness and enhance services for **transportation-disadvantaged** persons	◑	50
Training, employment, and education	32. Multiple **employment** and **training** programs: providing information on colocating services and consolidating administrative structures could promote efficiencies	◑	51
	33. **Teacher quality**: proliferation of programs complicates federal efforts to invest dollars effectively	◑	53
	34. Fragmentation of **financial literacy** efforts makes coordination essential	◑	54

Legend:

● = Addressed, meaning all actions needed in that area were addressed.

◑ = Partially addressed, meaning at least one action needed in that area showed some progress toward implementation, but not all actions were addressed.

○ = Not addressed, meaning none of the actions needed in that area were addressed.

Source: GAO analysis.

As noted above, table 2 presents GAO's assessment of the overall progress made in addressing the 47 cost-saving and revenue-enhancing areas.

GAO-12-453SP Follow-up on 2011 Report

Mission	Areas identified	Assessment	Page
Agriculture	35. Reducing some **farm program payments** could result in savings from $800 million over 10 years to up to $5 billion annually	○	56
Defense	36. DOD should assess costs and benefits of **overseas military presence** options before committing to costly personnel realignments and construction plans, thereby possibly saving billions of dollars	◐	57
	37. Total compensation approach is needed to manage significant growth in **military personnel costs**	◐	58
	38. Employing best management practices could help DOD save money on its **weapon systems acquisition programs**	◐	59
	39. More efficient management could limit future costs of **DOD's spare parts** inventory	◐	60
	40. More comprehensive and complete cost data can help DOD improve the cost-effectiveness of **sustaining weapon systems**	◐	61
	41. Improved **corrosion prevention** and control practices could help DOD avoid billions in unnecessary costs over time	◐	63
Economic development	42. Revising the **essential air service** program could improve efficiency	◐	64
	43. Improved design and management of the **universal service fund** as it expands to support broadband could help avoid cost increases for consumers	◐	66
	44. The **Corps of Engineers** should provide Congress with project-level information on **unobligated balances**	◐	67
Energy	45. Improved management of federal **oil and gas resources** could result in approximately $1.8 billion over 10 years[a]	◐	68
General government	46. Efforts to address **governmentwide improper payments** could result in significant cost savings	◐	70
	47. Promoting **competition for** the over $500 billion in **federal contracts** could potentially save billions of dollars over time	◐	71
	48. Applying **strategic sourcing** best practices throughout the federal procurement system could saves billions of dollars annually	◐	72
	49. Adherence to new guidance on **award fee contracts** could improve agencies' use of award fees to produce savings	◐	73
	50. Agencies could realize cost savings of at least $3 billion by continued disposal of **unneeded federal real property**	◐	74
	51. Improved cost analyses used for making **federal facility ownership** and **leasing** decisions could save tens of millions of dollars	◐	75
	52. The Office of Management and Budget's **IT Dashboard** reportedly has already resulted in $3 billion in savings and can further help identify opportunities to invest more efficiently in information technology	◐	76
	53. Increasing **electronic filing** of individual income **tax returns** could reduce IRS's processing costs and increase revenues by hundreds of millions of dollars	◐	77
	54. Using **return on investment** information to better target IRS enforcement could reduce the tax gap; for example, a 1 percent reduction would increase tax revenues by $3 billion[b]	◐	78

Mission	Areas identified	Assessment	Page
	55. Better management of **tax debt collection** may resolve cases faster with lower IRS costs and increase debt collected	◑	79
	56. Broadening IRS's authority to correct **simple tax return errors** could facilitate correct tax payments and help IRS avoid costly, burdensome audits	○	80
	57. Enhancing **mortgage interest information** reporting could improve tax compliance	○	81
	58. More information on the types and uses of canceled debt could help IRS limit revenue losses of **forgiven mortgage debt**	◑	82
	59. Better information and outreach could help increase revenues by tens or hundreds of millions of dollars annually by addressing overstated **real estate tax deductions**	◑	83
	60. Revisions to content and use of **Form 1098-T** could help IRS enforce higher education requirements and increase revenues	◑	84
	61. Many options could improve the tax compliance of **sole proprietors** and begin to reduce their $68 billion portion of the tax gap	○	85
	62. IRS could find additional **businesses not filing tax returns** by using third-party data, which show such businesses have billions of dollars in sales	◑	86
	63. Congress and IRS can help **S corporations** and their shareholders be more tax compliant, potentially increasing tax revenues by hundreds of millions of dollars each year	◑	87
	64. IRS needs an agencywide approach for addressing tax evasion among the at least 1 million **networks of businesses** and related entities	◑	88
	65. Opportunities exist to improve the targeting of the $6 billion **research tax credit** and reduce forgone revenue	○	89
	66. Converting the **new markets tax credit** to a grant program may increase program efficiency and significantly reduce the $3.8 billion 5-year revenue cost of the program	○	90
	67. Limiting the tax-exempt status of certain **governmental bonds** could yield revenue	○	91
	68. Adjusting **civil tax penalties** for inflation potentially could increase revenues by tens of millions of dollars per year, not counting any revenues that may result from maintaining the penalties' deterrent effect	◑	92
	69. IRS may be able to systematically identify **nonresident aliens** reporting unallowed tax deductions or credits	●	93
	70. Tracking **undisbursed balances** in **expired grant accounts** could facilitate the reallocation of scarce resources or the return of funding to the Treasury	○	94
Health	71. Preventing billions in **Medicaid improper payments** requires sustained attention and action by CMS	◑	95
	72. Federal oversight over **Medicaid supplemental payments** needs improvement, which could lead to substantial cost savings	○	96
	73. Better targeting of **Medicare's** claims review could reduce **improper payments**	◑	97
	74. Potential savings in **Medicare's payment** for **health care**	◑	98

Mission	Areas identified	Assessment	Page
Homeland security/ Law enforcement	75. **DHS's management of acquisitions** could be strengthened to reduce cost overruns and schedule and performance shortfalls	◐	100
	76. Improvements in **managing research and development** could help reduce inefficiencies and costs for homeland security	◐	102
	77. Validation of **TSA's behavior-based screening** program is needed to justify funding or expansion	◐	104
	78. More efficient **baggage screening systems** could result in about $470 million in reduced TSA personnel costs over the next 5 years	◐	106
	79. Clarifying availability of certain **customs fee collections** could produce a one-time savings of $640 million	◐	107
Income security	80. **Social Security** needs data on pensions from noncovered earnings to better enforce **offsets** and ensure benefit fairness, estimated to result in $2.4-$2.9 billion savings over 10 years	○	108
International affairs	81. Congress could pursue several options to improve collection of **antidumping** and **countervailing duties.**	○	109

Legend:

● = Addressed, meaning all actions needed in that area were addressed.

◐= Partially addressed, meaning at least one action needed in that area showed some progress toward implementation, but not all actions were addressed.

○ = Not addressed, meaning none of the actions needed in that area were addressed.

Source: GAO analysis.

[a]The Department of the Interior, Bureau of Land Management, updated the anticipated revenues from $1.75 billion to $1.8 billion in its fiscal year 2012 budget justification.

[b]The net tax gap was updated in 2012 and estimated to be $385 billion for the 2006 tax year. Thus, a 1 percent reduction would increase tax revenues by $3.8 billion.

Enclosure II: Progress Update for Each of the 176 Actions Needed within the 81 Areas

Overall assessment

Action 1

The Office of Management and Budget (OMB) in consultation with the relevant agencies should develop a governmentwide performance plan for food safety that includes results-oriented goals and performance measures and a discussion of strategies and resources.

Partially addressed ◑

Action 2

Congress should consider commissioning the National Academy of Sciences or a blue ribbon panel to conduct a detailed analysis of alternative food safety organizational structures.

Not addressed ○

Action 3

Congress should consider enacting comprehensive risk-based food safety legislation.

Not addressed ○

For more information, contact Lisa Shames at (202) 512-3841 or shamesl@gao.gov.

See GAO-11-318SP Actions Needed

Agriculture

1. Fragmented **food safety** system has caused inconsistent oversight, ineffective coordination, and inefficient use of resources

Action 1 progress

OMB participates in the President's Food Safety Working Group, created in March 2009, to coordinate federal efforts and set food safety goals to make food safer. OMB and the federal agencies that have food safety responsibilities have not developed a plan to improve coordination and provide a comprehensive picture of, or performance measures for, the federal government's food safety efforts. However, governmentwide coordination may be fostered by the provisions of the FDA Food Safety Modernization Act that require interagency coordination, including the preparation of certain reports and plans.[1] For example, in April 2011, the Department of Health and Human Services (HHS) issued its first annual report on interagency coordination and cooperation on food safety inspections, as required by the act. In addition, in December 2011 the Food Safety Working Group released a report describing the steps it has taken over the past 2 years to improve food safety, its plans for the next year, and how the agencies are coordinating on these efforts. Taken together, these reports by HHS and the Food Safety Working Group are first steps that may help address interagency coordination on food safety and inform a governmentwide plan.

Action 2 progress

No legislative action identified.

Action 3 progress

The FDA Food Safety Modernization Act, which was signed into law in January 2011, is intended to strengthen a major part of the food safety system, but does not apply to the entire federal food safety system or create a new risk-based food safety structure. The law does, however, include several sections that require interagency coordination on food safety oversight in areas such as inspections, seafood safety, and food imports.

---

[1]Pub. L. No. 111-353 (2011).

Overall assessment

Action 1

The Department of Defense (DOD) could take action to further assess alternatives for restructuring the governance structure of the military health care system.

Partially addressed

Defense

2. Realigning DOD's **military medical command** structures and consolidating common functions could increase efficiency and result in projected savings ranging from $281 million to $460 million annually[2]

Action 1 progress

In June 2011, the Deputy Secretary of Defense commissioned a task force to provide a report that includes an assessment of the governance of the military health system as a whole and in multi-service medical markets. This review was completed in September 2011, but the final report, with recommendations, has not been officially released. According to senior DOD officials, this report will be used as the basis for a report required by the National Defense Authorization Act for Fiscal Year 2012;[3] however, the act did not establish a completion date for the report. Specifically, the act requires the Secretary of Defense to submit to Congress a report that includes, among other things, a description of options developed and considered for the military health system's governance model, analysis of the strengths and weaknesses of each option, and estimated costs savings of each option, if any. The act also mandated that the Comptroller General conduct a detailed review of those governance options, and report on that review to Congress not later than 180 days after the submission of the Secretary of Defense's report. The act restricts the ability of the Secretary of Defense to restructure or reorganize the military health system until 120 days after the Comptroller General's report is submitted.

For more information, contact Brenda S. Farrell at (202) 512-3604 or FarrellB@gao.gov.

See GAO-11-318SP Actions Needed

[2]CNA's Center for Naval Analyses developed the savings estimates, and GAO adjusted the estimates from 2005 to 2010 dollars.
[3]Pub. L. No. 112-81, § 716 (2011).

Overall assessment

Action 1

The Department of Defense (DOD) needs to perform its own analysis of options aimed at potential consolidations and increased efficiencies in streamlining its urgent needs entities and processes. This analysis should carefully weigh the advantages and disadvantages of the options identified to determine the optimal course of action.

Partially addressed

Defense

3. Opportunities exist for consolidation and increased efficiencies to maximize response to **warfighter urgent needs**

Action 1 progress

In March 2011, DOD began an evaluation of the department's processes for the rapid fielding of capabilities in response to urgent operational needs, as required by the Ike Skelton National Defense Authorization Act for Fiscal Year 2011;[4] however, the department has not yet completed its evaluation. According to the department, this evaluation, which was due in January 2012, will be delivered later in 2012 and will examine areas of duplication identified by GAO, evaluate the potential for consolidations, and describe specific policy actions implemented to improve the department's overall urgent needs processes. DOD officials also noted other actions it has taken, including the establishment of a senior-level working group in June 2011 to provide oversight of DOD-wide efforts to fulfill urgent needs. Also, DOD issued guidance in January 2012, in part to standardize the definition of an urgent operational need.

For more information, contact Cary Russell at (404) 679-1808 or russellc@gao.gov.

See GAO-11-318SP Actions Needed

---

[4] *See* Pub. L. No. 111-383, § 804(a) (2011) (10 U.S.C. § 2302 note).

Overall assessment

Action 1

The Department of Defense's (DOD) senior leadership, to include the Deputy Secretary of Defense, should consider what actions the department can take to assure that the Joint Improvised Explosive Device Defeat Organization (JIEDDO) can centrally collect information and coordinate efforts, and whether it should enhance its tools to ensure all information on departmentwide counter-improvised explosive device (IED) programs is centrally collected and evaluated to limit unnecessary duplication, overlap, and fragmentation.

Partially addressed

For more information, contact Cary Russell at (404) 679-1808 or russellc@gao.gov.

See GAO-11-318SP Actions Needed

Defense

4. Opportunities exist to avoid unnecessary redundancies and improve the coordination of **counter-improvised explosive device efforts**

Action 1 progress

JIEDDO is currently developing a new information technology architecture, and plans to develop a database for counter-IED efforts across DOD as part of this new architecture. However, this effort is in the conceptualization stage, and DOD officials do not anticipate completion before the end of fiscal year 2012. Further, according to JIEDDO, in early 2012 DOD plans to revise the directive establishing JIEDDO to require the services and DOD agencies to report counter-IED initiatives to JIEDDO.

Overall assessment

Defense

5. Opportunities exist to avoid unnecessary redundancies and maximize the efficient use of **intelligence, surveillance,** and **reconnaissance** capabilities

Action 1

The Department of Defense (DOD) could develop an integrated intelligence, surveillance, and reconnaissance architecture, including manned and unmanned systems, to align departmentwide strategic goals.

Partially addressed

Action 1 progress

DOD is designing an intelligence, surveillance, and reconnaissance architecture, called the "Defense Intelligence Information Enterprise," to provide a common framework of tools for security and intelligence sharing. DOD plans to begin implementing the Defense Intelligence Information Enterprise framework in fiscal year 2013 and intends to revise its departmentwide strategic goals in its next intelligence, surveillance, and reconnaissance strategic plan.

Action 2

DOD could continue to develop tools— such as the Joint Staff's decision support tool—and performance measures to inform investment decisions.

Partially addressed

Action 2 progress

DOD continues to explore collaborative portfolio management tools that capture operational needs and consider the measured or projected performance of intelligence, surveillance, and reconnaissance systems. The Office of the Under Secretary of Defense for Intelligence is collaborating with the Joint Staff to enhance their developmental decision support tool to address operational requirements and inform investment decisions across its intelligence enterprise. DOD has not yet completed development of this tool. In addition, DOD plans to develop and include performance metrics in its 2012 strategic plan.

Action 3

DOD could establish linkages between intelligence, surveillance, and reconnaissance acquisition plans and strategic goals to better inform investment decisions.

Partially addressed

Action 3 progress

Recent agreements between the Director of National Intelligence and the Under Secretary of Defense (Intelligence) have resulted in the creation of the Consolidated Intelligence Guidance, which is expected to help synchronize investments between the Director of National Intelligence and DOD. According to DOD, this guidance, issued for fiscal year 2012, is goal-based and is designed to improve effectiveness in managing the shorter-term decisions in future defense budgets, acquisition plans, and investment decisions. DOD officials stated that this guidance has resulted in better alignment of investments with strategic goals. DOD plans to explicitly address the linkages between strategic goals and planned investments in the next intelligence, surveillance, and reconnaissance strategic plan scheduled for release in spring 2012.

Action 4

DOD could develop and enforce commonality and interoperability standards for sharing of intelligence, surveillance, and reconnaissance data and establish timelines for implementation.

Partially addressed

Action 4 progress

DOD stated that it is developing new methodologies for intelligence information sharing, such as the Distributed Common Ground/Surface System, to facilitate integration of intelligence capabilities, provide tools and systems that can work together to fulfill mission requirements, and share information among war fighting and coalition partners. DOD officials stated that the department plans to include standards for information sharing and timelines for information sharing in its new Defense Intelligence Information Enterprise framework.

For more information, contact Brian Lepore at (202) 512-4523 or leporeb@gao.gov.

See GAO-11-318SP Actions Needed

Overall assessment

Action 1

The Department of Defense (DOD) needs to complete its planned departmentwide tactical wheeled vehicle strategy to determine (1) what capabilities the Joint Light Tactical Vehicle will have, (2) the scope and cost of any recapitalization of other vehicles or production effort, and (3) the sustainment cost of placing the Mine Resistant Ambush Protected family of vehicles in its force structures. DOD should include in the strategy a cost-benefit analysis that could minimize the collective acquisition and support costs of the various tactical wheeled vehicle programs and reduce the risk of unplanned overlap or duplication.

Partially addressed

Defense

6. A departmentwide acquisition strategy could reduce DOD's risk of costly duplication in purchasing **Tactical Wheeled Vehicles**

Action 1 progress

DOD has taken steps to begin implementing this action; however, the department has not completed a tactical wheeled vehicle strategy or conducted a cost-benefit analysis for the acquisition and support costs of various programs. The Office of the Under Secretary of Defense for Acquisition, Technology, and Logistics has initiated a Ground Vehicle Portfolio Review, through which it plans to develop a unified, comprehensive, long-term tactical wheeled vehicle strategy that describes to key stakeholders how DOD plans to acquire and sustain an operationally relevant fleet. According to DOD officials, the portfolio review is planned to be continuous; outputs will support relevant program milestone decisions and annual program reviews, and will be closely coordinated with the service strategies. Phase 1 of the portfolio review, which is intended to build a comprehensive description of the current Tactical Wheeled Vehicle and Ground Combat Vehicle fleets, is under way. Milestones for subsequent phases will be established during Phase 1. Subsequent phases of the portfolio review should benefit from the knowledge resulting from planned near-term decisions, including budget decisions, regarding Joint Light Tactical Vehicle capabilities, High Mobility Multipurpose Wheeled Vehicle recapitalization, sustainment of the Mine Resistant Ambush Protected family of vehicles, and budgeted acquisition and support costs associated with those vehicles. In addition, the Army and Marine Corps updated their individual tactical wheeled vehicle strategies in January 2011 and June 2011, respectively.

Additionally, in March 2011, as directed by the Senate Armed Services Committee, both services provided congressional defense committees with acquisition strategies and plans for recapitalizing their respective High Mobility Multipurpose Wheeled Vehicle fleets. These plans are currently under review in light of the department's ongoing work to align strategic priorities and its budget.

For more information, contact Belva Martin at (202) 512-4841 or martinb@gao.gov.

See GAO-11-318SP Actions Needed

Overall assessment

Action 1

The Secretary of Defense should direct the Under Secretary of Defense for Acquisition, Technology, and Logistics, in coordination with the Chairman of the Joint Chiefs of Staff, to strengthen the Department of Defense's (DOD) joint oversight of its prepositioned stocks through such actions as clarifying lines of authority and reporting between the joint prepositioning working group and other components within DOD.

Partially addressed

Action 2

The Secretary of Defense should direct the Chairman of the Joint Chiefs of Staff and the Secretaries of the military services to synchronize at a departmentwide level, as appropriate, the services' prepositioning programs so that they include updated requirements and maximize efficiency in managing prepositioned assets and activities across the department to reduce unnecessary duplication.

Partially addressed

Action 3

The Secretary of Defense should direct the Office of the Under Secretary of Defense for Policy to develop strategic guidance that includes planning and resource priorities, linking the department's current and future needs for prepositioned stocks to evolving national defense objectives.

Not addressed ○

For more information, contact Cary Russell at (404) 679-1808 or russellc@gao.gov.

See GAO-11-318SP Actions Needed

Defense

7. Improved joint oversight of DOD's **prepositioning programs** for equipment and supplies may reduce unnecessary duplication

Action 1 progress

DOD has taken some actions to strengthen joint oversight of prepositioned stocks. For example, DOD broadened membership of its Global Prepositioning Materiel Capabilities Working Group to include a core member from the Office of the Under Secretary of Defense for Policy, the office responsible for developing related departmentwide prepositioned stocks strategy. DOD has also added joint staff representatives to this group. However, additional action is needed to codify lines of authority and reporting between the working group and DOD components.

Action 2 progress

DOD officials have stated that the department is examining opportunities to synchronize DOD prepositioning efforts as part of two ongoing departmentwide studies to determine how to manage prepositioned stocks. One study was planned for completion in the fall of 2011, but has not yet been released. According to a DOD official, the other study is projected for completion in 2012. However, DOD has not yet completed updating its requirements or identifying specific ways that prepositioned assets can be managed more efficiently.

Action 3 progress

No executive action taken.

Overall assessment

Defense

8. **DOD's business systems** modernization: opportunities exist for optimizing business operations and systems

Action 1

The Department of Defense (DOD) needs to develop supporting component architectures and align them with its corporate architecture to complete the federated business enterprise architecture.

Partially addressed

Action 1 progress

DOD continues to release updates to its corporate enterprise architecture, but the architecture has yet to be federated through development of aligned subordinate architectures for each of the military departments. In this regard, each of the military departments has made progress in managing its respective architecture program. For example, each department has established or is in the process of establishing an executive committee with responsibility and accountability for the enterprise architecture. However, there are still limitations in the scope and completeness, as well as the maturity of the military department architecture programs. For example, no military department has fully developed an enterprise architecture methodology or a well-defined business enterprise architecture and transition plan to guide and constrain business transformation initiatives.

In April 2011, DOD's Deputy Chief Management Officer issued a memorandum that requires integration of end-to-end business models and use of common standards for the development of the Business Enterprise Architecture and all subordinate architectures that federate or assert compliance with the Business Enterprise Architecture. While DOD recently drafted a technical transition plan that describes a vision for how standards will benefit the implementation of and ensure compliance with the Business Enterprise Architecture, the department has yet to finalize this plan or provide additional details for the plan's execution with associated timelines and metrics.

Action 2

DOD should leverage its federated architecture to avoid investments that provide similar but duplicative functionality in support of common DOD activities.

Not addressed

Action 2 progress

DOD has taken minimal steps to avoid duplicative investments, and it has yet to develop a well-defined federated architecture along with well-defined investment management policies and procedures that it could use to manage the thousands of business systems in a consistent, repeatable, and effective manner and that, among other things, maximizes mission performance while minimizing or eliminating system overlap and duplication. DOD officials have stated that operational activities identified by programs in its systems repository can be compared by the investment review boards to identify those activities that are 100 percent identical. However, this process depends on self-reported data from the programs, and there is little validation or verification of the information. DOD officials have also stated that they are working on selecting tools that, along with their adoption of common business process modeling standards, will allow them to compare activities proposed in a new investment to activities and services defined in the architecture. However, success of this type of tool depends on the amount of activities and services defined in the architecture, and the department has more work to do in this area. For example, DOD has identified 15 business processes to be defined in the Business Enterprise Architecture; however, only 2 of these processes will be fully defined by the end of fiscal year 2012.

8. **DOD's business systems** modernization (continued)

Action 3

DOD should work to institutionalize its business systems investment process at all levels of the organization.

Partially addressed

Action 3 progress

DOD continues to establish investment management processes, but neither department-level organizations nor the military departments have institutionalized the full range of project-level and portfolio-based information technology investment management policies and procedures that are necessary to meet the investment selection and control provisions of the Clinger-Cohen Act of 1996.[5] Specifically, GAO found that the DOD enterprise, Air Force, and Navy have yet to fully define 56 percent of the project-level practices, and Army has yet to do so for 78 percent of the practices.[6] With regard to the portfolio-level practices, DOD enterprise, Air Force, and Navy have yet to fully define 80 percent, and Army has yet to do so for any of the practices. For example, while DOD and the military departments have a process that calls for investments to be, among other things, compliant with DOD's Business Enterprise Architecture and economically justified, this process does not specify how the investment review boards are to use the full range of cost, schedule, and benefit data in making selection (i.e., certification) decisions.

Action 4

DOD must ensure that effective system acquisition management controls are implemented on each business system investment.

Partially addressed

Action 4 progress

DOD has taken steps to increase acquisition oversight for some business system modernization investments, but ensuring that effective system acquisition and management controls are implemented on each business system investment continues to remain a formidable challenge. GAO continues to identify weaknesses in such areas as architectural alignment, informed investment decision making, earned value management, economic justification, risk management, requirements management, and test management.[7] In February 2011, the milestone decision authority for major business systems (except for logistics) was delegated to the Deputy Chief Management Officer, who was also given authority to assign an overarching integrated product team lead to coordinate preparation for acquisition decisions. This change in policy should provide the Deputy Chief Management Officer with increased acquisition insight and control for several of the largest business systems modernization investments, which include key enterprise resource programs that account for billions of dollars of development funding intended to transform DOD's business operations. Further, in June 2011, the Under Secretary of Defense for Acquisition, Technology, and Logistics established a policy requiring the use of the Business Capabilities Lifecycle as the acquisition process for defense business systems modernizations with a total cost of over $1 million. While the Business Capabilities Lifecycle is intended to divide system development into discrete, fully-funded, and manageable increments to facilitate development and implementation, it is too early to determine the extent to which this new process will improve acquisition management controls. An independent risk assessment for major investments was developed to provide information to milestone decision authorities before major milestone decisions. According to officials, four such reviews have occurred in the last 2 years. However, DOD has not fully demonstrated how these risk assessments have influenced investment decision makers.

---

[5] 40 U.S.C. §§ 11311-11313.

[6] GAO, *Department of Defense: Further Actions Needed to Institutionalize Key Business System Modernization Management Controls*, GAO-11-684 (Washington, D.C.: June 29, 2011).

[7] GAO-11-684 and GAO, *High-Risk Series: An Update*, GAO-11-278 (Washington, D.C.: February 2011).

For more information, contact Valerie C. Melvin at (202) 512-6304 or melvinv@gao.gov.

See GAO-11-318SP Actions Needed

Overall assessment

Action 1

The Departments of Commerce, Housing and Urban Development, and Agriculture, and the Small Business Administration need to further utilize promising practices for enhanced collaboration. The actions that the four agencies should consider include seeking more opportunities for resource-sharing across economic development programs with shared outcomes, and identifying ways to leverage each program's strengths to improve their existing collaborative efforts.

Partially addressed

Action 2

The Departments of Commerce, Housing and Urban Development, and Agriculture, and the Small Business Administration need to collect accurate and complete data on program outcomes and use the information to assess each program's effectiveness.

Not addressed O

Economic Development

9. The efficiency and effectiveness of fragmented economic development programs are unclear

Action 1 progress

Three of the four agencies have taken initial steps to implement at least one of the collaborative practices that GAO has previously identified to administer their economic development programs.[8] For example, in April 2010 the U.S. Department of Agriculture (USDA) and the Small Business Administration (SBA) signed a memorandum of understanding (MOU) in response to GAO's recommendation that defined and articulated a common outcome focused on improving service delivery to small businesses in underserved rural areas. Under the MOU, USDA and SBA agreed that their field offices would advise potential borrowers of the other agency's programs that may meet their small business financing needs and coordinate the referral of small business applicants to one another where appropriate, work to make each agency's programs more complementary by minimizing differences in program fees and processing and closing procedures, and develop joint training seminars on each agency's programs. In addition, USDA and SBA agreed to measure progress under the MOU. USDA's April 2011 survey of state directors indicates progress under the MOU in several areas, including field offices advising borrowers of SBA's programs, referring borrowers to SBA and its resource partners, and exploring ways to make USDA and SBA programs more complementary. The Department of Commerce (Commerce) also provided information on its collaborative efforts with other federal agencies. For example, according to Economic Development Administration (EDA) officials, the agency has led an interagency effort called the i6 Challenge, which leverages resources from multiple federal agencies, with the common goal of spurring commercialization and manufacturing. The Department of Housing and Urban Development (HUD) has not taken similar steps to define and articulate common outcomes with other federal agencies. Moreover, HUD, USDA, and SBA have provided limited evidence that they have taken steps to develop compatible policies or procedures with other federal agencies, or to search for opportunities to leverage physical and administrative resources with their federal partners.

Action 2 progress

The four agencies have made minimal progress to collect more accurate and complete data on the outcomes for each of their economic development programs and to use the information to assess the effectiveness of each program. However, each agency has recently provided information on its plans to address this action. For example, EDA is developing a new performance management logic model to help EDA understand how various inputs, activities, outputs, and outcomes lead the agency to its desired vision of economic growth and prosperity. In addition, HUD officials told us that the department has plans for improving the quality of data for its Community Development Block Grant (CDBG) programs. In fiscal year 2012, HUD plans to fund improvements to its Integrated Disbursement and Information System; these improvements are intended to improve HUD's ability to track the progress of CDBG grantees in implementing activities and gather improved performance data. Similarly, according to USDA officials, the Rural Business Program office is in the process of updating its policies, procedures, and program guidelines in an effort to improve the accuracy and reliability of its program data. Finally, according to SBA officials, its Offices of International Trade and Entrepreneurial Development are implementing processes to capture outcomes for their respective programs.

---

[8]GAO, *Opportunities to Reduce Potential Duplication in Government Programs, Save Tax Dollars, and Enhance Revenue,* GAO-11-318SP (Washington, D.C.: Mar. 2, 2011).

9. Economic development programs (continued)

Additional work to assess progress in collaboration and evaluation could identify areas for improvement, consolidation, or elimination. More analysis is needed by the Departments of Commerce, Housing and Urban Development, and Agriculture, and the Small Business Administration and the Office of Management and Budget to determine the actual amount of duplicative spending in programs that are designed to target similar economic development activities, locations, and applicants.

Not addressed ○

No executive action taken.

For more information, contact William B. Shear at (202) 512-8678 or shearw@gao.gov.

See GAO-11-318SP Actions Needed

Overall assessment

Action 1

A fundamental re-examination and reform of the nation's surface transportation policies is needed. GAO has identified a number of principles that can help guide Congress in re-examining and reforming the nation's surface transportation policies. These principles include ensuring the federal role is defined based on identified areas of national interest and goals, incorporating accountability for results by entities receiving federal funds, employing the best tools and approaches to emphasize return on targeted federal investment, and ensuring fiscal sustainability. Applying these principles to a re-examination and reform of surface transportation programs would potentially result in a more clearly defined federal role in relation to other levels of government and thus a more targeted federal role focused around evident national interests.

Partially addressed

For more information, contact Susan Fleming at (202) 512-2834 or FlemingS@gao.gov.

See GAO-11-318SP Actions Needed

Economic Development

10. The federal approach to **surface transportation** is fragmented, lacks clear goals, and is not accountable for results

Action 1 progress

Comprehensive legislative action has not been taken to fundamentally re-examine the nation's surface transportation policies. However, several congressional committees have approved bills to reauthorize and reform surface transportation programs. For example, the Senate Environment and Public Works Committee approved a bill on November 9, 2011, reauthorizing the highway portion of the surface transportation program.[9] This bill contains measures to increase accountability for results by entities receiving federal funds and consolidate federal programs. In addition, the House Transportation and Infrastructure Committee approved a bill on February 2, 2012, that includes consolidating or eliminating a number of programs.[10] When GAO completed its work for this report, floor action was pending in the Senate. GAO is evaluating the extent to which ongoing legislative actions better define federal roles and goals, incorporate accountability for results, emphasize return on federal investment, and ensure fiscal sustainability.

---

[9] S. 1813, 112th Cong. (2011).
[10] H.R. 7, 112th Cong. (2012).

Overall assessment

Economic Development

11. Fragmented federal efforts to meet water needs in the U.S.-Mexico border region have resulted in an administrative burden, redundant activities, and an overall inefficient use of resources

Action 1

Congress may wish to consider requiring federal agencies to establish an interagency mechanism or process, such as a task force on water and wastewater infrastructure, in the border region. Congress could direct a group or task force to conduct certain activities. Specifically, GAO suggested that a task force, in partnership with state and local officials, should leverage collective resources to identify needs within the border region and establish compatible and coordinated polices across relevant agencies, such as a coordinated process for the selection of projects, and standardize applications, environmental review requirements, and engineering requirements to the extent possible.

Not addressed ○

Action 1 progress

No legislative action identified.

In January 2012, officials from several of the federal agencies[11] said they are working to coordinate their efforts in the border region within the current statutory authorities that exist; however, GAO continues to believe that a task force would allow the agencies to better coordinate. GAO notes that the administration has established the White House Rural Council to coordinate federal funding provided to rural communities, which may provide the opportunity to coordinate agencies' infrastructure funding in the border region.

For more information, contact David C. Trimble at (202) 512-3841 or trimbled@gao.gov.

See GAO-11-318SP Actions Needed

[11]These federal agencies include the Environmental Protection Agency, the Department of Agriculture, the Department of Housing and Urban Development, the U.S. Army Corps of Engineers, the Department of Health and Human Service's Indian Health Service, the Department of Commerce's Economic Development Administration, and the Department of the Interior's Bureau of Reclamation.

Overall assessment

Action 1

Changes in existing laws could streamline the requirements and provide fleet managers with more flexibility in meeting goals.

Not addressed ⭕

Energy

12. Resolving conflicting requirements could more effectively achieve **federal fleet energy goals**

Action 1 progress

No legislative action identified.

However, there has been related executive branch action. In May 2011, the President issued additional directives for federal fleet managers in his *Presidential Memorandum on Federal Fleet Performance*. Among other activities, this memorandum directs that by the end of 2015, all light-duty federal fleet vehicle acquisitions must be alternative-fueled vehicles. According to Department of Energy officials, this order does not reconcile conflicting requirements that federal fleets increase use of alternative fuels, reduce petroleum use, and reduce greenhouse gas emissions or provide additional flexibility to fleet managers, but the order does require activities that will help meet existing requirements.

For more information, contact Susan Fleming at (202) 512-2834 or flemings@gao.gov.

See GAO-11-318SP Actions Needed

Overall assessment

Action 1

Congress may wish to consider whether revisions to the ethanol tax credit are needed. Options could include the following:

- Maintain the volumetric ethanol excise tax credit (VEETC) at current levels.

- Allow the VEETC to expire at the end of 2011.

- Reduce the VEETC as Congress did in the 2008 Farm Bill, when the ethanol tax credit was reduced from 51 cents to 45 cents per gallon.

- Phase out the VEETC over a number of years.

- Modify the VEETC to counteract fluctuations in other commodities that can influence ethanol production, such as changes in crude oil prices. For instance, the ethanol tax credit could increase when crude oil prices are low and decrease when crude oil prices are high.

Addressed

For more information, contact Frank Rusco at (202) 512-3841 or ruscof@gao.gov

See GAO-11-318SP Actions Needed

Energy

13. Addressing duplicative federal efforts directed at increasing **domestic ethanol production** could reduce revenue losses by more than $5.7 billion annually

Action 1 progress

Congress allowed the VEETC to expire at the end of 2011. The most recent extension of the credit—set at 45-cents-per-gallon in the Tax Relief, Unemployment Insurance Reauthorization, and Job Creation Act of 2010[12]— expired on December 31, 2011. Fuel blenders that purchase and blend ethanol with gasoline no longer receive the credit.

---

[12]Pub. L. No. 111-312 (2010).

Overall assessment

14. Enterprise architectures: key mechanisms for identifying potential overlap and duplication

Action 1

Agencies should measure and report enterprise architecture results and outcomes (e.g., costs avoided through eliminating duplicative information technology investments).

Partially addressed ◖

Action 1 progress

The majority of the enterprise architecture efforts of the 27 agencies GAO reviewed can still be viewed as a work in progress, with much remaining to be accomplished. Since we reported in March 2011 that the Department of the Interior demonstrated that it had used enterprise architecture to avoid costs, an additional 4 agencies have measured and reported financial benefits from their respective enterprise architecture programs:

- Department of Agriculture expects to save $27 million over 5 years (2011 through 2015) by moving 120,000 e-mail users to a cloud-based solution.
- Department of Defense, Office of the Secretary, described in its April 2011 Congressional Report on Defense Business Operations about $179 million in financial savings between fiscal years 2008 and 2010 by streamlining Navy business operations, retiring legacy systems, and moving toward a real-time paperless business environment that reduces time and costs for processing vendor payments.
- Nuclear Regulatory Commission achieved an estimated $1.3 million cost avoidance in 2011 by eliminating duplicative staff planning systems.
- Department of Health and Human Services saved about $21 million while sustaining increased network usage in fiscal year 2011 by moving to a new telecommunications contract, which was facilitated by its enterprise architecture program.

Twelve agencies reported financial benefits; however, they did not reliably measure them (i.e., they did not provide supporting documentation):

- Department of Commerce;
- Department of Education;
- Department of Energy;
- Department of Homeland Security;
- Department of Justice;
- Department of Transportation;
- Office of Personnel Management;
- General Services Administration;
- Small Business Administration;
- Social Security Administration;
- Department of the Army; and
- Department of State.

An additional 10 agencies did not report financial benefits, although 8 of these agencies reported that they have established or expect to establish a process to measure benefits in the future:

- Department of the Air Force;
- Department of Housing and Urban Development;
- Department of Labor;
- Department of the Navy;
- Department of the Treasury;
- Department of Veterans Affairs;
- Environmental Protection Agency;
- National Aeronautics and Space Administration;
- National Science Foundation; and
- U.S. Agency for International Development.

For more information, contact David A. Powner at (202) 512-9286 or pownerd@gao.gov.

See GAO-11-318SP Actions Needed

Overall assessment

General Government

15. Consolidating **federal data** centers provides opportunity to improve government efficiency

---

Action 1

It will be important for individual agencies to move quickly to correct any missing items in their plans, establish sound baselines so that progress and efficiencies can be measured, begin their consolidation efforts, track their progress, and report to the Office of Management and Budget (OMB) on their progress over time.

Partially addressed

Action 1 progress

The administration's Implementation Plan to Reform Information Technology, dated December 2010, identifies steps and milestones to (1) consolidate at least 800 federal data centers by 2015, and (2) establish a governmentwide marketplace for data center availability in 2012.

In July 2011, OMB required the 24 federal agencies participating in the Federal Data Center Consolidation Initiative to complete their consolidation plans. Beginning in October 2011, all of the agencies posted their updated plans online. GAO has ongoing work assessing the completeness of these plans. A preliminary analysis shows that not all agency plans have been updated to include all required information.

In December 2011, the Federal Chief Information Officer (CIO) announced that the definition of a data center had been expanded from facilities over 500 square feet to one that includes data centers of all sizes. This change resulted in an expanded data center baseline of 3,133 centers, an increase from the 2,094 centers originally reported by agencies. The Federal CIO reported that agencies planned to close 525 of these centers by the end of calendar year 2012 and 1,080 by the end of 2015. The Federal CIO also announced a further goal of closing 40 percent, or at least 1,200, of the 3,133 centers.

Action 2

OMB should work with agencies to establish goals and targets for consolidation (both in terms of cost savings and reduced data centers), maintain strong oversight of the agencies' efforts, and look for consolidation opportunities across agencies.

Partially addressed ◐

Action 2 progress

The Analytical Perspectives for the President's budget for fiscal year 2012 also addresses data center consolidation. It notes the importance of the federal data center consolidation effort and identifies for each of the 24 participating agencies, the number of data centers in 2010, as well as the agencies' 2015 consolidation targets.

As noted above, in July 2011, OMB required the 24 federal agencies participating in the Federal Data Center Consolidation Initiative to complete their consolidation plans, including required information on consolidation savings and goals. Beginning in October 2011, all of the agencies posted their updated plans online. GAO has ongoing work assessing the extent to which agencies have updated this required information. A preliminary analysis shows that not all agency plans have been updated to include all required information. GAO also has ongoing work assessing OMB's continuing oversight of the consolidation initiative.

OMB also has a planned initiative to look for consolidation opportunities across agencies. Specifically, it plans to develop a governmentwide marketplace for data center availability in 2012. Further, OMB has developed a cost model for agencies to use to estimate consolidation cost savings.

OMB's continued oversight of agencies' data center consolidation efforts will help better ensure that the federal consolidation initiative meets its cost savings and data center reduction targets.

For more information, contact David Powner at (202) 512-9286 or pownerd@gao.gov.

See GAO-11-318SP Actions Needed

Overall assessment

General Government

16. Collecting improved data on **interagency contracting** to minimize duplication could help the government leverage its vast buying power

Action 1

The Office of Management and Budget (OMB) will need to fully implement the steps it is taking to address identified shortcomings in the management of interagency contracting.

Partially addressed

Action 1 progress

OMB is working with agencies to improve data on interagency contracting, and some actions are in the early stages of implementation. OMB notes that continued investment in centralized procurement data systems is required in order to sustain improvements in the collection and use of procurement data, including data on interagency contracts, and that the first phase of a centralized data system, called the System for Award Management, is scheduled to be launched in May 2012. OMB's Office of Federal Procurement Policy (OFPP) provided an update describing actions it is taking to address identified shortcomings in the management of interagency contracting. In particular, OFPP noted that it is working with agencies to update current data on interagency contracts. OFPP also noted that it may not be necessary to create a new database on interagency contracts because much of this information is already available. OFPP plans to notify agencies of a new page on OMB's budget information Web site with links to information on existing interagency contract vehicles, new multiagency contracts, and new multiagency blanket purchase agreements. OFPP still needs to decide on the need to create a centralized database containing this information.

Action 2

The General Services Administration (GSA) will need to fully implement the steps it is taking to address identified shortcomings in the management of interagency contracting.

Partially addressed

Action 2 progress

GSA has prepared an action plan that addresses identified shortcomings in the management of interagency contracting, but the action plan has not yet been fully implemented. GSA has completed a high-level analysis of options for collecting transactional data on orders through the Multiple Award Schedule program and plans to implement and evaluate a pilot program for collecting this information.

Action 3

Improvements are still needed regarding the accuracy of the federal contracts database in order to determine whether the contracts are being used in an efficient and effective manner.

Addressed

Action 3 progress

OFPP has worked with agencies to ensure that data in the Federal Procurement Data System are accurate and complete, including a random sampling of fiscal year 2010 contract actions, which reflected a 96.5 percent accuracy rate. OFPP also established an interagency procurement data quality working group to review various efforts agencies are employing to improve data quality and leverage successful efforts across the acquisition community.

Action 4

Require business case analyses for new multiagency contracts.

Addressed

For more information, contact William T. Woods at (202) 512-4841 or WoodsW@gao.gov.

See GAO-11-318SP Actions Needed

Action 4 progress

On September 29, 2011, the Administrator of OFPP issued a memorandum that provided guidance for development of a business case analysis for certain interagency contracts, including new multiagency contracts.[13] In addition, on January 3, 2012, a final rule was issued amending the Federal Acquisition Regulation to require a business case analysis to support the creation of certain of these contracts.[14]

---

[13]OFPP Memorandum, "*Development, Review and Approval of Business Cases for Certain Interagency and Agency-Specific Acquisitions*" (Sept. 29, 2011).
[14]77 Fed. Reg. 183 (Jan. 3, 2012).

Overall assessment

General Government

17. Periodic reviews could help identify ineffective **tax expenditures** and redundancies in related tax and spending programs, potentially reducing revenue losses by billions of dollars

Action 1

The Director of the Office of Management and Budget (OMB) in consultation with the Secretary of the Treasury should present tax expenditures in the budget together with related outlay programs.

Not addressed ◯

Action 1 progress

No executive action taken. OMB did not agree with this recommendation and favors reporting tax expenditures separately from the rest of the budget. Although OMB had begun presenting tax expenditure sums alongside outlays and credit activity for each budget function in the federal budget from fiscal year 1998 through fiscal year 2002, OMB discontinued the practice. Tax expenditures were not integrated in the President's fiscal year 2012 budget.

Action 2

The Director of OMB in consultation with the Secretary of the Treasury should develop and implement a framework for conducting performance reviews of tax expenditures. This includes (1) outlining leadership responsibilities and coordination among agencies with related responsibilities; (2) setting a review schedule; (3) identifying review methods and ways to address the lack of credible tax expenditure performance information; and (4) identifying resources needed for tax expenditure reviews.

Not addressed ◯

Action 2 progress

The Director of OMB has not developed a framework for reviewing tax expenditure performance. The President's fiscal year 2012 budget stated that developing an evaluation framework is a significant challenge and that the administration's focus is on addressing challenges with data availability and analytical constraints so that the administration can work towards crosscutting analyses examining tax expenditures alongside related spending programs; however, no timetable or specifics were included. In January 2012, OMB officials stated that the President's fiscal year 2012 budget proposed numerous reforms to tax expenditures, which it estimated would save billions in total; published evaluations supporting the proposals were not available.

Action 3

The Director of OMB in consultation with the Secretary of the Treasury should develop guidance on incorporating tax expenditures in agencies' strategic plans and performance reports.

Not addressed ◯

Action 3 progress

OMB guidance has not explicitly addressed how agencies should incorporate tax expenditures in strategic plans and annual performance plans and reports. Moving forward, the GPRA Modernization Act of 2010 (GPRAMA)[15] calls for a more coordinated approach to focus on results and improve government performance. OMB, in coordination with agencies, is to develop a limited number of outcome-oriented, crosscutting policy goals and indicates that it will identify the relevant agencies and federal activities—including tax expenditures—that contribute to each crosscutting goal. OMB has issued some guidance to help agencies implement GPRAMA, and OMB plans to address tax expenditures in guidance forthcoming in 2012.

---

[15]Pub. L. No. 111-352 (2011).

17. Tax expenditures (continued)

Action 4

The Director of OMB in consultation with the Secretary of the Treasury should require that tax expenditures be included in Executive Branch budget and performance review processes.

Not addressed ○

Action 4 progress

OMB has not made progress on systematically including tax expenditures along with related outlay programs in the Executive Branch's budget and performance review processes. The President's fiscal year 2012 budget stated that the Administration will be working towards examining the objectives and effects of the wide range of tax expenditures in the budget, though no timetable or specifics were provided.

Effective GPRAMA implementation could help inform reexamination or restructuring efforts and lead to more efficient and economical service delivery in overlapping program areas by identifying the various agencies and federal activities—including tax expenditures—that contribute to crosscutting outcomes. As noted above, OMB has stated that forthcoming OMB GPRAMA guidance will address tax expenditures.

For more information, contact Michael Brostek at (202) 512-9110 or brostekm@gao.gov.

See GAO-11-318SP Actions Needed

Overall assessment

Health

18. Opportunities exist for **DOD** and **VA** to jointly modernize their **electronic health record systems**

Action 1

The Secretaries of Defense and Veterans Affairs should revise the departments' joint strategic plan to include information discussing their electronic health record system modernization efforts and how those efforts will address the departments' common health care business needs.

Partially addressed

Action 1 progress

The Departments of Defense (DOD) and Veterans Affairs (VA) have taken steps to discuss and improve their electronic health record system capabilities, but they have not yet revised their joint strategic plan to include these efforts or indicate how they will address common health care business needs. The Secretaries of DOD and VA have met to discuss their respective departments' efforts to pursue joint development and acquisition of integrated electronic health record (iEHR) capabilities. Among other things, the Secretaries have established the departments' interagency program office as the single point of accountability for the development and implementation of the iEHR, while also improving their efforts to further implement joint health information technology (IT) capabilities at DOD and VA's first fully integrated health care center in North Chicago, Illinois. The departments plan further action to address this area. Specifically, DOD and VA intend to issue an addendum to their joint strategic plan for fiscal years 2011 through 2013 that is to include objectives and goals related to the departments' iEHR efforts.

Action 2

The Secretaries of Defense and Veterans Affairs should further develop the departments' joint health architecture to include their planned future state and transition plan from their current state to the next generation of electronic health record capabilities.

Partially addressed

Action 2 progress

The DOD and VA have taken steps toward developing a joint health architecture, but the architecture is not sufficiently mature and the departments have not defined how they intend to transition from their current architecture to a planned future state. The Secretaries of DOD and VA agreed in May 2011 that the departments would implement a common architecture for the iEHR. The departments have since developed, and the Secretaries have approved, a high-level representation of the "to be" architecture for the iEHR. In addition, the interagency program office is to facilitate further development and maintenance of the iEHR architecture in conjunction with the departments' Health Executive Council and the recently established Health Architecture Review Board. Nevertheless, DOD and VA have not yet fully developed a joint health architecture that includes a plan for transitioning from their current state to the next generation of electronic health record capabilities.

Action 3

The Secretaries of Defense and Veterans Affairs should define and implement a process, including criteria that considers costs, benefits, schedule, and risks, for identifying and selecting joint IT investments to meet the departments' common health care business needs.

Partially addressed

Action 3 progress

The Secretaries of DOD and VA have agreed to develop a process for identifying and selecting joint IT investments; however, the departments have not yet implemented this process. Specifically, both Secretaries have agreed to develop and implement the iEHR and they have approved a governance structure that defines how they intend to accomplish this effort. This structure includes the departments themselves, which have responsibility for establishing their respective health care requirements; joint forums such as the Health Executive Council, which is to collaborate with the interagency program office to collect the requirements; and the program office itself, which is to identify the IT investments to meet the requirements. However, the departments have not yet implemented this process.

For more information, contact Valerie C. Melvin at (202) 512-6304 or melvinv@gao.gov.

See GAO-11-318SP Actions Needed

Overall assessment

19. **VA** and **DOD** need to control **drug** costs and increase **joint contracting** wherever it is cost-effective

Action 1

The Department of Veterans Affairs (VA) and the Department of Defense (DOD) should analyze whether greater cost savings could be achieved through joint contracting for brand name drugs than are currently achieved through their independent strategies, and determine whether it would be cost-effective to take steps to resume joint contracting for brand name drugs.

Partially addressed

Action 1 progress

Neither DOD nor VA indicated that either agency intended to analyze whether it would be cost-effective to resume joint contracting for brand name drugs. However, in January 2012, the agencies indicated that they are coordinating on joint contracting opportunities for brand name drugs through the Contracting Subcommittee of the VA Federal Pharmacy Executive Steering Committee, whose purpose is to coordinate federal pharmacy activities across federal agencies. For example, in November 2011, VA and DOD entered into a joint contract for a brand name drug, and VA reported that it would continue its practice of coordinating with DOD on opportunities for contracts for brand name drugs. However, according to DOD officials, there was evidence from VA and DOD's joint contracting experience that joint contracting does not necessarily result in lower prices for either or both agencies. DOD cited past experiences in which the agencies did not receive a single bid in response to some large joint generic drug contract solicitations. DOD also noted that differences in the design of VA's and DOD's pharmacy benefits programs make cost-effective opportunities, as currently designed, for brand-name drug joint contracts less common than they were prior to DOD's fiscal year 2005 implementation of its uniform formulary process.

Action 2

DOD should identify, implement, and monitor efforts to control retail pharmacy spending, an area for which drug spending is increasing and cannot be controlled through joint contracting efforts.

Addressed

Action 2 progress

DOD reported that a number of initiatives to control retail pharmacy costs had been identified and implemented, and that it continues to monitor its cost control efforts.

- As a result of applying federal pricing arrangements—which generally result in prices lower than retail prices—to drugs dispensed at retail pharmacies, DOD reported that as of July 31, 2011, DOD had received $2.7 billion in manufacturer refunds for fiscal years 2009, 2010, and 2011.
- DOD reported that its uniform formulary process has ensured use of the most clinically- and cost-effective agents at all three points of pharmacy service through the use of formulary management tools such as step therapy. For example, DOD reported that step therapy for cholesterol lowering agents implemented in May 2010 enabled DOD to save approximately $82.8 million in the first year after implementation. The 3-year cost avoidance projection for this class of drugs is $141.6 million.
- Also, in January 2010, DOD implemented an in-depth communications plan to promote the use of a less costly pharmacy option. DOD officials told GAO that this effort has resulted in higher use of the less-expensive TRICARE Mail Order Pharmacy venue and savings to the government, which they estimate to be over $30 million in 2010. Additionally, DOD reports that an adjustment to prescription drug copayments, effective October 1, 2011, will further encourage the use of the TRICARE Mail Order Pharmacy and should result in additional savings.

Action 3

VA and DOD should continue their efforts to jointly contract for generic drugs, and look for opportunities to increase joint contracting efforts as generic versions of existing brand name drugs become available.

Addressed

For more information, contact Randall B. Williamson at (202) 512-7114 or williamsonr@gao.gov.

See GAO-11-318SP Actions Needed

19. VA and DOD drug costs and joint contracting (continued)

Action 3 progress

VA continues to collaborate with DOD to identify opportunities for joint contracting for generic drugs through the Federal Pharmacy Executive Steering Committee. Additionally, DOD noted in January 2012 that joint contracts had been awarded for several generic drugs that had previously been "blockbuster" brand name drugs, and additional joint contract negotiations were under way.

Overall assessment

О

Action 1

The Secretary of Health and Human Services should develop and implement a strategic plan that defines goals, objectives, and priorities for establishing an electronic public health situational awareness network. Such a plan should include performance measures for evaluating capabilities of existing and planned information systems. The strategic plan should integrate related strategies and information technology initiatives within the Department of Health and Human Services (HHS) for sharing information among federal, state, local, and tribal entities.

Not addressed О

Health

20. HHS needs an overall strategy to better integrate nationwide **public health information** systems

Action 1 progress

HHS has not finalized a strategic plan for establishing an electronic nationwide public health situational awareness network. HHS officials with the Office of the Assistant Secretary for Preparedness and Response stated that they intend to release an Implementation Plan for the National Health Security Strategy. This plan is to incorporate a strategy for integrating the goals and objectives of the various offices' disparate plans to implement information systems in support of the nationwide public health situational awareness network capabilities required by section 202 of the Pandemic and All-Hazards Preparedness Act.[16] Although HHS intended to release the Implementation Plan in early 2011, it has not yet done so. Department officials stated that they now expect to release the plan in early 2012.

For more information, contact Valerie C. Melvin at (202) 512-6304 or melvinv@gao.gov.

See GAO-11-318SP Actions Needed

---

[16]42 U.S.C. § 247d–4(d). The act requires that a strategic plan be submitted to congressional committees no later than June 18, 2007, and that the electronic nationwide public health situational awareness network be established no later than December 19, 2008.

GAO-12-453SP Follow-up on 2011 Report

Overall assessment

Action 1

The Homeland Security Council should consider establishing a focal point to coordinate federal biodefense activities, including biosurveillance.

Partially addressed

Action 2

The overarching biodefense enterprise would benefit from strategic oversight mechanisms, including a national strategy, to ensure efficient, effective, and accountable results.

Not addressed ○

Homeland Security / Law Enforcement

21. Strategic oversight mechanisms could help integrate fragmented interagency efforts to defend against **biological threats**

Action 1 progress

In August 2011, the National Security Staff (NSS), which supports the Homeland Security Council, stated that two of its directorates serve as focal points to coordinate federal biodefense activities, as suggested in GAO's March 2011 report. However, the NSS did not provide any details about how these directorates will provide the strategic and integrated oversight of the entire biodefense enterprise, which GAO reported was lacking.

Action 2 progress

NSS officials stated that they are overseeing the development of a national strategy for biosurveillance, but that strategy has not yet been developed and does not cover the full biodefense enterprise. In August 2011, the NSS indicated that two of its directorates are overseeing the development of the strategy. However, the NSS did not provide a timeline for completing these actions. The strategy also would not address the overarching biodefense enterprise, as GAO previously recommended.

For more information, contact William O. Jenkins, Jr., at (202) 512-8777 or jenkinswo@gao.gov.

See GAO-11-318SP Actions Needed

Overall assessment

Action 1

The Department of Homeland Security (DHS) should provide guidance and oversight for interagency forums—which include both Integrated Border Enforcement Team (IBET) and Border Enforcement Security Task Force (BEST) interagency forums—to help prevent duplication of effort and help efficiently utilize personnel resources to strengthen DHS's coordination efforts along the northern border.

Not addressed ○

Action 2

As DHS establishes a mechanism for determining the benefits of participating in the IBET and BEST interagency forums, DHS could lead efforts to develop a framework for identifying the costs incurred by all partners participating in each forum.

Not addressed ○

For more information, contact Rebecca Gambler at (202) 512-6912 or GamblerR@gao.gov.

See GAO-11-318SP Actions Needed

Homeland Security / Law Enforcement

22. DHS oversight could help eliminate potential duplicating efforts of interagency forums in **securing** the **northern border**

Action 1 progress

No executive branch action has been taken.

Draft legislation has been introduced in Congress that would require DHS to consider whether the establishment of a new interagency forum would duplicate an existing forum's effort; the bill, however, has yet to be enacted and does not address duplication among existing interagency forums. On March 3, 2011, the Jaime Zapata Border Enforcement Security Task Force Act was introduced in Congress.[17] This draft bill would provide authorization of appropriations to establish and operate a BEST program in areas designated by the Secretary of Homeland Security. The House Homeland Security Committee approved the bill, as amended, by voice vote on September 21, 2011, and the bill was officially reported out of committee on November 4, 2011. The bill, as amended, requires the Secretary to consider whether an IBET already exists in an area under consideration for establishment of a BEST unit. However, the bill does not specifically discuss addressing areas of overlap or duplication among existing IBETs and BEST units.

Action 2 progress

No executive action taken.

---

[17]H.R. 915, 112th Cong. (as reported by H.R. Comm. on Homeland Security, Nov. 4, 2011).

GAO-12-453SP Follow-up on 2011 Report

Overall assessment

Action 1

Continually monitoring the actions planned by the Department of Justice (Justice); the Bureau of Alcohol, Tobacco, Firearms, and Explosives (ATF); and the Federal Bureau of Investigation (FBI) in four areas of explosives investigations—including jurisdiction, explosives training, shared explosives databases, and laboratories—could help Justice ensure the successful implementation of those actions to reduce duplication and overlap and to improve coordination.

Addressed

Homeland Security / Law Enforcement

23. The Department of Justice plans actions to reduce overlap in **explosives investigations**, but monitoring is needed to ensure successful implementation

Action 1 progress

Executive branch action has been taken in each of the four identified areas where duplication and redundant efforts needed to be addressed.

Jurisdiction: To address jurisdictional disputes in explosives investigations, as of May 2011, Justice created a National Explosives Task Force where ATF and FBI are collocated in headquarters. This task force monitors explosives investigations, may determine the lead agency in investigations when there is uncertainty among field agents, and ensures that ATF and FBI are coordinating.

Training: To address fragmentation in the explosives training provided by ATF and FBI, the two agencies created a joint curriculum for their post-blast training as of May 2011. According to ATF and FBI, the new curriculum has resulted in both agencies providing consistent information to the agents and state and local bomb squads whom they train. They are also considering creating other joint curricula in areas such as homemade explosives.

Explosive database: To ensure that both agencies are aware of explosives incidents, ATF released a more user friendly version of the Bomb and Arson Tracking System—an explosives incident reporting system—in May 2011. Both ATF and FBI have issued new protocols requiring agents to enter explosives incidents into the Bomb and Arson Tracking System. In addition, both the ATF and FBI are requiring that all explosives incidents be reported to their respective Strategic Information Operation Centers (SIOC). The SIOCs will notify each other when an incident is reported. In addition, explosives incidents are also reported to the National Explosives Task Force. According to ATF and FBI, these multiple reporting mechanisms ensure that both ATF and FBI are aware of all explosives incidents and that the incidents are entered in the Bomb and Arson Tracking System.

Explosive laboratories: To better leverage their explosives forensic capabilities, according to officials, ATF and FBI laboratories meet on a regular basis to discuss options where coordination can be increased. According to ATF and FBI officials, both laboratories are at capacity, but they have agreed to utilize a joint lab information management system and joint training of laboratory staff. DOJ plans to lay out implementation steps during fiscal year 2012.

Additionally, according to ATF and FBI officials, the Office of the Deputy Attorney General meets regularly with ATF and FBI to monitor their progress and address any potential concerns. This coordination is important to help ensure that the above improvements are sustained.

For more information, contact Eileen Larence at (202) 512-6510 or LarenceE@gao.gov .

See GAO-11-318SP Actions Needed

Overall assessment

Action 1

The Transportation Security Administration (TSA) and the Federal Motor Carrier Safety Administration (FMCSA) could improve interagency coordination by sharing each other's schedules for conducting future security reviews, and avoid scheduling reviews on hazardous material trucking companies that have recently received, or are scheduled to receive, a review from the other agency. TSA could also discontinue conducting voluntary security reviews on hazardous material trucking companies, thereby enabling TSA to increase its security efforts in other areas.

Addressed

Action 2

TSA could request that the full results of past FMCSA security reviews of trucking companies be provided through an existing Department of Transportation (DOT) Web portal. Doing so would require cooperation from FMCSA.

Not addressed O

Action 3

TSA and FMCSA should continue efforts toward the long-term goal of TSA assuming full regulatory responsibility from FMCSA for commercial trucking security, thereby reducing fragmentation.

Partially addressed

For more information, contact Steve Lord at (202) 512-4379 or lords@gao.gov.

See GAO-11-318SP Actions Needed

Homeland Security / Law Enforcement

24. TSA's security assessments on commercial trucking companies overlap with those of another agency, but efforts are under way to address the overlap

Action 1 progress

In August 2011, TSA reported that the agency had discontinued conducting security reviews on trucking companies that are covered by the FMCSA program. Discontinuing such reviews should eliminate the short-term overlap between TSA and FMCSA's reviews of hazardous material trucking companies.

Action 2 progress

No executive action taken. In January 2012, TSA reported that due, in part, to data subscription costs, the agency had decided to discontinue access to FMCSA's data for hazardous material trucking companies until TSA has full regulatory oversight in this area. TSA officials had previously reported that the agency would have little use for FMCSA data until TSA assumes such regulatory responsibility, and said the data are limited to FMCSA-related regulations and do not provide information about a carrier's overall security preparedness. TSA officials also reported that they are confident that FMCSA would provide TSA with security review results for individual motor carriers if security conditions warrant such a request. However, GAO continues to believe that utilization of FMCSA's security information in the DOT Web portal could benefit TSA because a considerable amount of the data in FMCSA's review is the same or similar to the data TSA was previously collecting. In addition, FMCSA conducts approximately 1,800 security reviews per year. TSA officials said that they were not in a position to estimate when the regulations will be issued and thus did not know when TSA would assume full regulatory responsibility from FMCSA.

Action 3 progress

In October 2011, TSA reported that the agency had drafted proposed regulations for hazardous material trucking security, which would give TSA regulatory responsibility for this area, and that the proposed regulations were undergoing TSA review. TSA officials did not have an estimate for when the regulations would be issued and thus did not know when TSA would assume full regulatory responsibility from FMCSA.

Overall assessment

Action 1

The Department of Homeland Security (DHS) and Transportation Security Administration (TSA) could identify and implement ways to more efficiently share security-related information by assessing the various mechanisms available to public transit agencies— including DHS's information network, TSA's portal on the network, and the public transit analysis center—as well as the information they provide, and identify opportunities to streamline these mechanisms.

Partially addressed

Action 2

DHS could develop and track verifiable cost data specific to each of its information-sharing mechanisms, as part of TSA's streamlining and financial management efforts. Developing such baseline cost data could assist TSA in identifying potential cost savings resulting from the consolidation of these mechanisms and provide opportunities for the agency to better allocate its information-sharing resources.

Not addressed

For more information, contact Steve Lord at (202) 512-4379 or LordS@gao.gov.

See GAO-11-318SP Actions Needed

Homeland Security / Law Enforcement

25. DHS could streamline mechanisms for **sharing security-related information** with **public transit agencies** to help address overlapping information

Action 1 progress

TSA helped launch a new report that streamlines and shares security-related information among public transit agencies, but security-related information has yet to be fully incorporated from all three mechanisms that GAO identified as potentially duplicative. In February 2011, TSA, in coordination with federal and industry stakeholders through an information-sharing working group, launched the Transit and Rail Intelligence Awareness Daily (TRIAD) Report. The overall intent of the TRIAD is to streamline the analysis, share, and exchange intelligence and security information, and help public transit stakeholders more efficiently share information by reducing the number of e-mails that stakeholders receive, and the number of persons sending those e-mails. However, the TRIAD does not yet reference specific information from the DHS information network or TSA's portal on the network, although the working group has discussed doing so.

TSA officials reported that maintaining different information-sharing mechanisms is necessary at this time to ensure that the diversity of information is covered. However, GAO continues to believe that maintaining separate systems to provide similar information to similar user groups is not efficient and that this potential overlap could overwhelm public transit agencies with similar information. Until the information-sharing working group completes its efforts to filter security-related information obtained from all three mechanisms through the TRIAD, public transit agencies will continue to receive information from multiple sources, making it difficult for them to discern relevant security-related information.

Action 2 progress

No executive action taken.

Overall assessment

26. FEMA needs to improve its oversight of **grants** and establish a framework for assessing capabilities to identify gaps and prioritize investments

Action 1

The Federal Emergency Management Agency (FEMA) could benefit from examining its grant programs and coordinating its application process to eliminate or reduce redundancy among grant recipients and program purposes.

Partially addressed ◑

Action 1 progress

The Department of Homeland Security (DHS) has sought to consolidate several of FEMA's smaller grant programs within larger grant programs, but FEMA has not coordinated application reviews of grant projects across four of the largest preparedness grant programs, which have similar goals, fund similar types of projects, and are awarded in many of the same urban areas. DHS's fiscal year 2012 budget request, similar to its 2011 request, proposed the elimination of six stove-piped and duplicative stand-alone grant programs, consolidating them into broader grants awarded to states and localities based on risk. This approach would provide greater flexibility for state and local officials to fill critical homeland security capability gaps and would significantly streamline the application process. Specifically, the President's fiscal year 2012 budget proposed to incorporate some of the smaller grant programs as allowable expenses within the larger programs. For instance, investments previously funded under the Driver's License Security Grant Program, the Citizen Corps Grant Program, and the former Interoperable Emergency Communications Grant Program would be treated as allowable expenses under the State Homeland Security Grant Program. The consolidated appropriations act for fiscal year 2012 appropriated a lump sum of $1.35 billion for FEMA preparedness grant programs, allowing DHS to determine the distribution among the various grant programs.[18] However, four of the largest preparedness grant programs, which have similar allowable costs, are being reviewed by two separate divisions, and FEMA has not yet developed a mechanism to coordinate the review of grant project applications internally to identify unwarranted overlap and mitigate the potential for unnecessary duplication across grant applications. According to FEMA officials, the agency plans to phase in a new grants management system, which is scheduled for completion by fiscal year 2014, to help, among other things, eliminate redundancies in its grants programs. However, it is not clear to what extent this new system will provide FEMA with the means to coordinate application reviews of its grant programs.

Additionally, *The Amateur Radio Emergency Communications Enhancement Act of 2011,* as reported out by the Senate Committee on Homeland Security and Governmental Affairs in June 2011, would require the DHS Inspector General to determine whether and to what degree FEMA grant programs provide duplicative or overlapping assistance, and make recommendations for the consolidation and elimination of grant programs to reduce duplication of assistance.[19]

---

[18]H.R. Rep. No. 112-331, at 175-77 (2011) (Conf. Rep.).
[19]S. 191, 112th Cong. (2011).

26. FEMA grants (continued)

Action 2

Congress may wish to consider limiting preparedness grant funding to maintaining existing capabilities (as determined by FEMA) until FEMA completes a national preparedness assessment of capability gaps at each level based on tiered, capability-specific performance objectives to enable prioritization of grant funding.

Partially Addressed ◑

Action 2 progress

In the continuing appropriations act for fiscal year 2011, Congress appropriated $875 million less for FEMA preparedness grants than the amount requested in the President's fiscal year 2011 budget.[20] Similarly, the consolidated appropriations act for fiscal year 2012 appropriated $1.7 billion for FEMA preparedness grants, $1.28 billion less than requested.[21] The Senate Committee report accompanying the DHS appropriations bill for fiscal year 2012 directs FEMA to develop guidance for grantees on best practices to manage current funding to ensure the most necessary capabilities are sustained. The report encourages FEMA to provide flexibility in grant expenditures to ensure the least amount of degradation to current capabilities occurs and directs the agency to brief the Committee quarterly on the specific processes being put in place to manage the grant programs in a way that promotes sustainability of current capacity.[22]

In December 2011, DHS officials said that they had not yet completed the development and implementation of the preparedness system (additional discussion of this issue is included below). However, in the interim, FEMA officials stated that FEMA has clarified grant guidance and reporting to support maintenance needed to sustain current capabilities in response to grantee concerns regarding allowable uses of grant funds.

Action 3

FEMA should complete a national preparedness assessment of capability gaps at each level based on tiered, capability-specific performance objectives to enable prioritization of grant funding, and FEMA could identify the potential costs for establishing and maintaining those capabilities at each level and determine what capabilities federal agencies should provide.

Not addressed ○

Action 3 progress

DHS has announced plans to develop and implement a national preparedness system that would enable it to assess these capability gaps, but the system remains under development. Therefore, actions on the assessment of capability gaps have not yet begun. In its May 2011, Implementation Plan for Presidential Policy Directive 8: National Preparedness, DHS announced plans to develop and implement a national preparedness system to provide an integrated approach to preparedness that can be implemented and measured at all levels of government to link together programs and requirements into a comprehensive system, driving rational decision making and allowing for a direct and defensible assessment of progress against clearly defined objectives. According to the plan, the national preparedness system will be based on a consistent methodology for assessing the threats and hazards that drive planning, including resource requirements, existing capabilities and capability gaps, and investments to close those gaps. FEMA officials described efforts they have underway, which are aimed at assessing state-level capabilities, that they said would provide a new baseline to meet or exceed several aspects of this action. However, FEMA has not yet begun to develop and implement a system to assess capability gaps on a national level.

---

[20]Pub. L. No. 112-10, § 1632 (2011).

[21]This total includes all grant programs in the state and local programs account and the Emergency Management Performance Grant program but does not include funding appropriated for firefighter assistance grant programs.

[22]S. Rep. No. 112-74, at 124 (2011).

Action 4

Once FEMA has completed its assessment, Congress may wish to consider limiting the use of federal preparedness grant programs to fund only projects that support the development of identified, validated, and documented capability gaps that may (or may not) include maintaining existing capabilities developed.

Not addressed ◯

Action 4 progress

Because FEMA has not yet completed its assessment, this suggested action cannot yet be considered by Congress.

For more information, contact William O. Jenkins, Jr. at (202) 512-8757 or jenkinswo@gao.gov.

See GAO-11-318SP Actions Needed

Overall assessment

Action 1

The U.S. Agency for International Development (USAID), in consultation with the Department of Defense (DOD) and other relevant U.S. agencies, should consider designating *Afghan Info* or some other database as the centralized U.S. government database for U.S. development efforts in Afghanistan. This database should, among other things, ensure that the information in the database (1) captures all agency development efforts and (2) is accessible to all U.S. government agencies involved in U.S.-funded development projects in Afghanistan.

Partially addressed

International Affairs

27. Lack of information sharing could create the potential for duplication of efforts between U.S. agencies involved in **development efforts** in **Afghanistan**

Action 1 progress

The *Afghan Info* database has been designated as the centralized database for U.S. development efforts in Afghanistan, but it does not readily capture relevant DOD data. On October 2, 2011, the Deputy Ambassador, U.S. Embassy Kabul, signed a memo requiring that all Embassy agencies and sections utilizing foreign assistance funds report information on their programs and projects into *Afghan Info*. Additionally, a November 2011 U.S. Status Report: Afghanistan and Pakistan Civilian Engagement issued by the Office of the Special Representative for Afghanistan and Pakistan and signed by the Secretary of State noted that Embassy Kabul is taking steps to utilize the *Afghan Info* database to capture all foreign assistance activities being implemented by U.S. government agencies. However, DOD's Commander's Emergency Response Program data is still not in the *Afghan Info* database. USAID has started discussions with DOD about how to get Commander's Emergency Response Program data into the database because, according to USAID, the Ambassador only has direct authority over Chief of Mission offices and agencies. USAID officials said that *Afghan Info* is in the process of being transitioned, by late February 2012, to an internet-based system that will allow all agencies access.

For more information, contact Charles Johnson at (202) 512-7331 or johnsoncm@gao.gov.

See GAO-11-318SP Actions Needed

Overall assessment

28. Despite restructuring, overlapping roles and functions still exist at State's **Arms Control** and **Nonproliferation Bureaus**

Action 1

The Department of State (State) should implement GAO's recommendations to formally delineate in the Foreign Affairs Manual (FAM) the roles of the two new bureaus.

Addressed

Action 1 progress

State updated the FAM in February and April 2011 to formally delineate the roles of the Bureau of Arms Control, Verification and Compliance and the Bureau of International Security and Nonproliferation. By making these improvements, State could reduce personnel and other overhead costs by helping address the multiple mission redundancies identified among the offices and functions of the new International Security and Nonproliferation and Arms Control, Verification, and Compliance bureaus.

Action 2

State should implement GAO's recommendations to direct that key transformation practices and steps be incorporated into the FAM.

Addressed

Action 2 progress

State updated the FAM in May 2011 to direct that, to the extent practicable, major reorganizations of bureaus or offices at State should follow GAO's key transformation practices. Such key practices include ensuring that top leadership drives the transformation and establishing a coherent mission and integrated strategic goals to guide the transformation.

For more information, contact Thomas Melito at (202) 512-9601 or melitot@gao.gov.

See GAO-11-318SP Actions Needed

Overall assessment

29. Actions needed to reduce administrative overlap among **domestic food assistance** programs

Action 1

The U.S. Department of Agriculture (USDA) should identify and develop methods for addressing potential inefficiencies and reducing unnecessary overlap among its smaller food assistance programs while ensuring that those who are eligible receive the assistance they need. These methods could include conducting a study as a first step; convening a group of experts; identifying which of the lesser-studied programs need further research and taking steps to fill the research gap; or identifying and piloting proposed changes.

Not addressed ◯

Action 1 progress

No executive action taken.

Action 2

USDA could broaden its efforts to simplify, streamline, or better align eligibility procedures and criteria across programs to the extent that it is permitted by law. Options such as consolidating or eliminating overlapping programs also have the potential to reduce administrative costs but may not reduce spending on benefits unless fewer individuals are served as a result.

Not addressed ◯

Action 2 progress

No executive action taken.

For more information, contact Kay E. Brown at (202) 512-7215 or brownke@gao.gov.

See GAO-11-318SP Actions Needed

Overall assessment

Social Services

30. Better coordination of federal **homelessness** programs may minimize fragmentation and overlap

Action 1

It will be important for the federal agencies that have adopted the Federal Strategic Plan to Prevent and End Homelessness (the Federal Strategic Plan) to develop implementation plans that include but are not limited to a project schedule, resource allocation, outreach measures, and a performance measurement strategy to evaluate their progress.

Partially addressed

Action 1 progress

While not all members of the U.S. Interagency Council on Homelessness (USICH) are expected to do so, the three key member agencies—the Departments of Health and Human Services (HHS), Housing and Urban Development (HUD), and Veterans Affairs (VA)—have either adopted or aligned their strategic plans with the Federal Strategic Plan, which was developed in 2010. GAO has ongoing audit work to determine the extent to which council member agencies have implementation plans in place and the extent to which those plans incorporate the recommended elements.

Action 2

Agencies need to improve collaborative efforts as outlined in the U.S. Interagency Council on Homelessness's (USICH) Federal Strategic Plan.

Partially addressed

Action 2 progress

Better collaboration is part of the mission of the USICH and one of the objectives of the Federal Strategic Plan. Collaborative steps have been taken by some agencies as they address the issue of homelessness, but not all agencies are as far along in the process. For example, HHS and VA have been working with HUD to better coordinate collection, analysis, and reporting of homelessness data within those three agencies. In addition, during fiscal year 2012, the USICH is facilitating discussions among and between agencies about the feasibility of creating a common data standard regarding housing stability across relevant federal programs. If adopted, such a common data standard would also allow for greater collaboration among agencies. Agencies have also stated that increased collaboration has occurred between both targeted and mainstream federal homelessness programs. For instance, Department of Agriculture officials stated that as a result of their involvement with USICH, they have begun to plan strategies with another agency to increase access to mainstream programs. However, providers GAO spoke with stated that greater collaboration of homelessness efforts is still needed among agencies, especially those that provide housing and health services. Providers acknowledged that coordination can be difficult because agencies are not set up to work together and coordination efforts take time and resources to be successfully implemented. Therefore, while agency actions to improve collaboration are in process, additional collaboration is still needed to further coordinate the federal response to homelessness. GAO is currently assessing agency efforts to improve collaboration and will report on this later this year.

For more information, contact Alicia Puente Cackley at (202) 512-8678 or cackleya@gao.gov

See GAO-11-318SP Actions Needed

Overall assessment

Social Services

31. Further steps needed to improve cost-effectiveness and enhance services for **transportation-disadvantaged** persons

Action 1

Federal departments on the Interagency Transportation Coordinating Council on Access and Mobility (Coordinating Council), including the Departments of Agriculture, Education, Health and Human Services, Housing and Urban Development, Interior, Labor, Transportation, and Veterans Affairs, should identify and assess their transportation programs and related expenditures and work with other departments to identify potential opportunities for additional coordination. The Coordinating Council should develop the means for collecting and sharing this information by establishing agency roles and responsibilities and developing a strategy to reinforce cooperation.

Partially addressed

Action 1 progress

The Department of Transportation, which is the head of the Coordinating Council, maintains a comprehensive inventory of its programs, but most participating federal departments do not have an inventory of existing programs or related expenditure information for transportation services and have not been actively working with other departments to identify potential opportunities for additional coordination. One of seven Coordinating Council working groups in fiscal year 2011, however, has identified a new opportunity to coordinate certain services for a targeted group of transportation-disadvantaged persons. As part of the Coordinating Council's Veteran's Affairs working group, the Departments of Health and Human Services, Labor, Transportation, and Veterans Affairs recently worked together to develop a Veteran's Transportation & Community Living Initiative, launched in July 2011. Through this initiative, the Federal Transit Administration has made over $34 million in Bus and Bus Facilities grant funding available to local governmental agencies to finance the capital costs of implementing, expanding, or increasing access to local One-Call/One-Click Transportation Resource Centers. In addition, a Web site exists (the Coordinating Council's United We Ride Web site) to collect and share program information, but the information provided does not comprehensively address all relevant transportation programs for transportation-disadvantaged persons.

Action 2

Federal departments on the Coordinating Council should develop and disseminate policies and grantee guidance for coordinating transportation services.

Partially addressed

Action 2 progress

Most federal departments on the Coordinating Council have not disseminated policies and grantee guidance for coordinating transportation services since March 2011. One of eight federal departments we reviewed, however, recently disseminated guidance for their grantees for coordinating transportation services. The Department of Labor's Employment and Training Administration and Office of Disability Employment Policy jointly issued a Training and Employment Notice on January 3, 2012 for the public workforce system on meeting employment-related transportation needs of businesses and job seekers. This guidance provides strategies for connecting individuals, including those with disabilities and other challenges, to employment with transportation to jobs and training.

For more information, contact David Wise at (202) 512-2834 or WiseD@gao.gov.

See GAO-11-318SP Actions Needed

Overall assessment

Action 1

The Secretaries of Labor and Health and Human Services should work together to develop and disseminate information that could inform efforts by states and localities in increasing administrative efficiencies in employment and training programs, including initiatives to consolidate program administrative structures and collocate new partners at one-stop centers.

Partially addressed

Training, Employment, and Education

32. Multiple **employment** and **training** programs: providing information on collocating services and consolidating administrative structures could promote efficiencies

Action 1 progress

According to department officials, the Departments of Labor (Labor) and Health and Human Services (HHS) are collaboratively pursuing efforts which may increase administrative efficiencies. These efforts include testing innovative strategies, developing technical assistance, and conducting joint evaluation activities. Department officials cited the following:

- Labor will be awarding competitive grants intended to improve services and job seeker and employer outcomes and lower costs or reduce program overlap and administrative cost;
- HHS and Labor have jointly developed and disseminated information through technical assistance to cross-agency teams to support the improvement of employment, training, and education outcomes for low-skilled adults; and
- HHS is collaborating with Labor to conduct an evaluation to better understand policies, practices, and service delivery strategies that lead to better alignment of the Workforce Investment Act and Temporary Assistance for Needy Families (TANF), including promising state and local practices for successful coordination between these programs.

As part of its proposed changes to the Workforce Investment Act, the President's fiscal year 2012 budget request proposed consolidating the Vocational Rehabilitation (VR) States Grants program, Supported Employment State Grants, Projects with Industry, Migrant and Seasonal Farmworkers, and the in-service training portion of VR Training program. The administration also proposed consolidating Education's Career and Technical Education-Basic Grants to States and Tech Prep Education programs, at the same time reducing program funding. According to an official at the Department of Education, the fiscal year 2012 appropriations[23] did not consolidate these programs. However, the fiscal year 2012 appropriation provided no funds for the Projects with Industry; provided funds to pay only the continuation costs of the Migrant and Seasonal Farmworkers program's current projects; and the fiscal year 2011 appropriation eliminated funding for Tech Prep, according to the official.

In addition, the administration proposed transferring the Senior Community Service Employment Program from Labor to HHS, while reducing the program's funding. According to a Labor official, the fiscal year 2012 appropriation did not transfer the program to HHS. There was a small reduction in funding relative to the fiscal year 2011 appropriation.

---

[23] Pub. L. No. 112-74 (2011).

GAO-12-453SP Follow-up on 2011 Report

Action 2

Labor and HHS should examine the incentives for states and localities to undertake initiatives in increasing administrative efficiencies in employment and training programs and, as warranted, identify options for increasing such incentives.

Partially addressed ◐

Action 2 progress

Labor reported that it will be awarding competitive grants to encourage states to (1) achieve outcomes for lower cost; (2) reduce program overlap and administrative costs; and (3) strengthen coordination and alignment across programs and funding streams. Part of this grant money will be made available through a pilot program that pays for services only after defined outcomes are achieved through effective, promising strategies, according to department officials. In addition, officials reported that Labor and HHS, along with other federal agencies, have been meeting to identify opportunities for promoting joint strategic planning across programs. Officials said the departments will be examining incentives for states and localities to undertake strategic planning across programs as a way to increase administrative efficiencies and alignment of core public workforce, as well as partner programs such as Temporary Assistance for Needy Families.

For more information, contact Andrew Sherrill at (202) 512-7252 or sherrilla@gao.gov.

See GAO-11-318SP Actions Needed

Overall assessment

Training, Employment, and Education

33. Teacher quality: proliferation of programs complicates federal efforts to invest dollars effectively

Action 1

The Secretary of Education should work with other agencies as appropriate to develop a coordinated approach for routinely and systematically sharing information that can assist federal programs, states, and local providers in achieving efficient service delivery.

Not addressed

Action 1 progress

No executive action taken. The Department of Education noted barriers to program alignment, such as programs with differing definitions for similar populations of grantees, which create an impediment to coordination.

Action 2

Congress could help eliminate some of the barriers to program alignment through legislation, particularly through the pending reauthorization of the Elementary and Secondary Education Act of 1965 (ESEA) and other key education bills. Specifically, Congress may choose either to eliminate programs that are too small to evaluate cost-effectively or combine programs serving similar target groups into a larger program.

Partially addressed

Action 2 progress

Two proposed bills currently pending before Congress would, in part, repeal provisions of the ESEA, as amended. The Setting New Priorities in Education Spending Act was introduced in the House on May 13, 2011, with the intended purpose of repealing ineffective or unnecessary education programs.[24] According to the committee reporting the bill, it would repeal the authorization for more than 40 education programs, some of which are related to teacher quality. In addition, the Senate Committee on Health, Education, Labor and Pensions reported an original bill, the Elementary and Secondary Education Reauthorization Act of 2011, on October 20, 2011, which would also repeal various ESEA provisions that may impact teacher quality programs.[25]

Action 3

Congress might also include legislative provisions to help the Department of Education reduce fragmentation, such as by giving broader discretion to the agency to move resources away from certain programs. Congress could provide the department guidelines for selecting these programs. To the extent that overlapping programs continue to be authorized, they could be better aligned with each other in a way that allows for comparison and evaluation to ensure they are complementary rather than duplicative.

Not addressed

Action 3 progress

No legislative action identified.

For more information, contact George A. Scott at (202) 512-7215 or scottG@gao.gov.

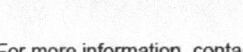

See GAO-11-318SP Actions Needed

---

[24]H.R. 1891, 112th Cong. (2011).

[25]Although this original bill has been reported out of the committee, as of January 27, 2012, it had not yet been introduced in the Senate and therefore does not have a bill number. For the text of the original bill, refer to http://www.help.senate.gov/hearings/hearing/?id=b4d24a56-5056-9502-5d73-a45a120b096b.

Overall assessment

34. Fragmentation of **financial literacy** efforts makes coordination essential

Action 1

The Financial Literacy and Education Commission should enhance its efforts to coordinate federal activities, such as by exploring further opportunities to strengthen its role as a central clearinghouse for federal financial literacy resources.

Partially addressed

Action 1 progress

If implemented, the Financial Literacy and Education Commission's 2011 National Strategy will address GAO's suggestion to strengthen the Commission's coordination and clearinghouse efforts. The strategy identifies coordination as one of five action areas and sets a goal of establishing a clearinghouse of federal research, best practices, and other information related to financial literacy. According to Commission staff, their goal is to initiate the clearinghouse in early 2012.

Action 2

The Office of Financial Education, within the Bureau of Consumer Financial Protection, and the Office of Financial Education and Financial Access, within the Department of the Treasury, will need to coordinate their roles and activities closely to avoid unnecessary overlap and make the most productive use of their respective resources.

Partially addressed

Action 2 progress

As the new Bureau of Consumer Financial Protection has been hiring staff and planning its financial education activities, it has been in regular communication with the Department of the Treasury. Department officials told us that the two agencies meet about once a month in an effort to coordinate their respective roles and activities. These coordination efforts are ongoing and not enough time has passed to assess their results.

Action 3

The Financial Literacy and Education Commission should build on progress it has made in recent years in promoting partnerships among the federal, state, local, nonprofit, and private sectors.

Partially addressed

Action 3 progress

The Financial Literacy and Education Commission's 2011 National Strategy and accompanying implementation plan discuss strategies for involving and working with nonfederal entities in achieving the commission's goals, but not enough time has passed to assess the execution of the National Strategy.

34. Financial literacy (continued)

Action 4

Federal agencies should measure the outcomes of their financial literacy efforts and federal financial literacy resources should be focused on those agencies and programs with the most expertise and best track records. The Financial Literacy and Education Commission and the Bureau of Consumer Financial Protection could potentially play a role in developing or disseminating a standard set of evaluation tools or benchmarks that would help assess which federal initiatives have the most effective outcomes.

Partially addressed

Action 4 progress

The 2011 National Strategy for Financial Literacy sets goals for encouraging evidence-based research and outcome-based program evaluation, although evaluation tools have yet to be completed and disseminated to federal agencies. The Financial Literacy and Education Commission's 2011 implementation plan includes developing a federal action plan for these goals and the Departments of the Treasury and Education have plans to share lessons learned from existing research with other federal agencies. However, the National Strategy does not make recommendations for allocating federal resources accordingly.

For more information, contact Alicia Puente Cackley at (202) 512-8678 or cackleya@gao.gov.

See GAO-11-318SP Actions Needed

Overall assessment

Action 1

Congress may wish to consider reducing or eliminating fixed annual payments to farmers, called direct payments, by (1) lowering payment or income eligibility limits; (2) reducing the portion of a farm's acres eligible for the payments; or (3) terminating or phasing out direct payments.

Not addressed ◯

For more information, contact Lisa Shames at (202) 512-3841or shamesl@gao.gov.

See GAO-11-318SP Actions Needed

Agriculture

35. Reducing some farm program payments could result in savings from $800 million over 10 years to up to $5 billion annually

Action 1 progress

No legislative action identified.

Overall assessment

Action 1

The Department of Defense (DOD) should conduct a comprehensive reassessment of its overseas presence, including the costs and benefits of various alternatives.

Partially addressed

Action 2

To address specific regional issues in Europe, DOD should reassess plans in Europe, including the costs and benefits of keeping Army brigades in Germany and the appropriateness of building a new Army headquarters given the potential changes in force structure.

Partially addressed

Action 3

To address specific regional issues in Africa, DOD should reassess missions of the combined joint task force in Djibouti as well as identifying the projected costs for the task force and, in concert with DOD or the Navy, developing a realistic funding plan for the task force's sustainability.

Partially addressed ◖

For more information, contact John Pendleton at (202) 512-3489 or pendletonj@gao.gov.

See GAO-11-318SP Actions Needed

Defense

36. DOD should assess costs and benefits of **overseas military presence** options before committing to costly personnel realignments and construction plans, thereby possibly saving billions of dollars

Action 1 progress

DOD has taken some steps that would facilitate such a reassessment, but has not completed a comprehensive reassessment of its overseas presence that includes the costs and benefits of alternatives. For example, DOD has instituted a global posture prioritization panel wherein the combatant commands, the services, the Office of the Secretary of Defense, and other relevant DOD organizations prioritize global posture initiatives collectively and do so in time for those initiatives that are selected to be included in each service's budget plan. In addition, DOD has issued guidance that requires combatant commands to report costs associated with planned projects in their respective posture plans but has not finalized the instruction that would implement this guidance.

Additionally, in the report accompanying the Senate bill for the National Defense Authorization Act for Fiscal Year 2012, the Senate Armed Services Committee discussed the importance of using an objective and transparent methodology to capture the full current cost and estimate the future cost of military overseas presence.[26] For example, the committee directed DOD to provide an update on its plans to implement GAO recommendations to more accurately and comprehensively account for costs related to overseas posture plans.

Action 2 progress

In January 2012, the administration announced that the Army will remove two brigade combat teams from Europe, but did not specify when this would occur. Also, DOD is considering increasing its naval presence overseas to meet ballistic missile defense requirements for the region. At present, DOD is assessing the cost and benefits of stationing naval forces in Spain to meet the requirement. According to DOD officials, the Department will provide an overview of planned changes to posture in Europe in its annual report to Congress on global defense posture in spring 2012.

Action 3 progress

DOD is taking steps to determine the future task force's presence in Djibouti and how it will be funded and sustained, but has not yet developed specific plans and funding estimates. DOD officials told GAO that U.S. Africa Command has assessed the need for the task force and determined the task force to be integral to the U.S. presence in East Africa through at least 2017, and that final decisions about specific needs will be made later in 2012 as part of the department's review of worldwide posture plans.

In a committee report, the Senate Appropriations Committee directed the Secretary of the Navy to submit a master plan that would include information on the planned facilities for Camp Lemonier in Djibouti. An annual update to the master plan is to be submitted to the defense committees with the budget submission,[27] which usually occurs in February each year. According to DOD officials, the Navy is currently conducting a facilities-planning effort and the department will submit the master plan to Congress in August 2012.

---

[26] See S. Rep. No. 112-26, at 191 (2011).
[27] See S. Rep. No. 112-29, at 12-13 (2011).

Overall assessment

Action 1

The Department of Defense (DOD) could recognize long-term cost avoidance by addressing in a compensation strategy what types of compensation are effective, and not incurring costs for compensation that may not be effective, in helping the department achieve its recruiting and retention goals.

Partially addressed

Defense

37. Total compensation approach is needed to manage significant growth in **military personnel costs**

Action 1 progress

DOD has taken some steps to determine the effectiveness of select special and incentive pays. For example, DOD employed a contractor to help develop a compensation analysis model for selected officer communities and anticipates using it, once completed, to help set effective compensation for those officer communities. In August 2011, DOD hired the RAND Corporation to develop and apply a model to analyze the effect of special and incentive pays on the staff of selected officer communities to ensure that staffing goals of the officer community can be met and that compensation is efficient. DOD officials anticipate that this analysis will be used to help the department and the services more efficiently use and set rates for special and incentive pay compensation to influence a member's retention decision. The study, entitled Officer Special and Incentive Pay Analysis, is ongoing and expected to be completed in August 2012.

To achieve additional progress on this action, DOD should continue analyzing special and incentive pays to determine the most efficient amount to offer to meet staffing goals, including expanding this study to include the enlisted servicemember population. While DOD's efforts to assess officers' special and incentive pays shows progress, special and incentive pays are one of many compensation tools that DOD uses to recruit and retain its active duty personnel. Further, special and incentive pays represented less than 5 percent of DOD's compensation costs for active duty personnel. To completely address GAO's action needed, DOD should assess the extent its other pays and benefits contribute to its recruiting and retention goals, and use this information to formulate a clear compensation strategy that includes performance measures.

For more information, contact Brenda S. Farrell at (202) 512-3604 or farrel b@gao.gov.

See GAO-11-318SP Actions Needed

Overall assessment

Defense

38. Employing best management practices could help DOD save money on its **weapon systems acquisition programs**

Action 1

The Department of Defense (DOD) could achieve significant cost savings by employing best management practices at all phases of its weapon system acquisition process—including early systems engineering, analyzing alternatives, managing changes in system requirements, and more prototyping early in programs development testing.

Partially addressed

Action 1 progress

DOD has made some progress in implementing several best practices on weapon system acquisition programs, but not all best practices are being applied by all acquisition programs and more consistent implementation is needed. For example, in March 2011, GAO reported that almost all of the 14 planned major defense acquisition programs reviewed intended to conduct early systems engineering reviews before starting development, but fewer are taking other actions, such as developing early prototypes, that could improve their chances of success.[28] GAO also reported in July 2011 that the military departments held configuration steering board meetings—a key mechanism for managing changes in system requirements—for 74 of 96 major defense acquisition programs they managed in 2010.[29] GAO made several recommendations to ensure that DOD holds configuration steering boards for all programs, and the department is planning to take action to address them.

Action 2

DOD has started the process of reviewing the potential cost of individual weapon system programs to meet warfighters' most pressing needs, but the department must still address the overall affordability of its major weapon system investment portfolio.

Partially addressed

Action 2 progress

DOD has started to address the affordability of its weapon programs on an individual basis, but not as a whole. DOD has started to implement its September 2010 guidance that requires "should cost" estimates and affordability targets be set for each new weapon system acquisition program.[30] However, in June 2011, GAO reported that DOD's process for validating new weapon system requirements still does not take into account a requirement's affordability or set priorities in a way that can be used to help manage DOD's overall weapon system investments.[31] In January 2012, DOD revised its requirements process to include joint prioritization, which should be a useful input for balancing weapon system investments.

Action 3

DOD needs to do a better job planning and executing programs on a day-to-day basis to achieve better outcomes. Critical to achieving successful outcomes is establishing and sustaining knowledge-based, realistic program baselines.

Partially addressed

Action 3 progress

DOD has made some progress in implementing, but has not yet fully adhered to, knowledge-based acquisition approaches. In March 2011, GAO reported that newer weapon programs are demonstrating higher levels of knowledge at key decision points, but most are still not fully adhering to a knowledge-based acquisition approach.[32]

For more information, contact Michael J. Sullivan at (202) 512-4841 or sullivanm@gao.gov.

See GAO-11-318SP Actions Needed

---

[28]GAO, *Defense Acquisitions: Assessments of Selected Weapon Programs,* GAO-11-233SP (Washington, D.C.; Mar. 29, 2011).

[29]GAO, *Defense Acquisitions: DOD Can Improve Its Management of Configuration Steering Boards,* GAO-11-640 (Washington, D.C.: July 7, 2011).

[30]"Should-cost" estimates are based on bottoms-up assessments of what programs should cost, if reasonable efficiency and productivity enhancements are undertaken. They can be used as a basis for contract negotiation and incentives.

[31]GAO, *DOD Weapon Systems: Missed Trade-off Opportunities During Requirements Reviews,* GAO-11-502 (Washington, D.C.: June 16, 2011).

[32]GAO, *Defense Acquisitions: Assessments of Selected Weapon Programs,* GAO-11-233SP (Washington, D.C.; Mar. 29, 2011).

Overall assessment

Action 1

The Department of Defense (DOD) could limit future costs by focusing its efforts on better managing on-order inventory. Specifically, DOD should focus on reducing on-order inventory levels that are not needed for current needs or projected demand.

Partially addressed

Action 2

DOD should address systemic weaknesses in demand forecasting, revise management practices to incorporate flexibility needed to minimize the impact of demand fluctuations, and track the cost efficiency of its inventory management processes.

Partially addressed

For more information, contact Zina Merritt at (202) 512-4300 or merrittz@gao.gov.

See GAO-11-318SP Actions Needed

Defense

39. More efficient management could limit future costs of **DOD's spare parts** inventory

Action 1 progress

DOD is in the process of implementing its November 2010 *Comprehensive Inventory Management Improvement Plan* (the Plan). In 2011, GAO found that DOD's Plan, which was required by the National Defense Authorization Act for Fiscal Year 2010 (Pub. L. No. 111-84, § 328), provides a comprehensive plan for improving inventory management systems of the military departments and the Defense Logistics Agency.[33] One of two goals in the Plan is to reduce the amount of on-order excess inventory[34] from 8.5 percent of on-order dollars above the approved acquisition objective across DOD for fiscal year 2009 to 6 percent in fiscal year 2014 and 4 percent in fiscal year 2016. Additionally, DOD and its components are in the process of reviewing and strengthening its approval and reporting procedures for on-order excess, which may result in needed updates to DOD and component policy and regulations. Implementation of the Plan is ongoing, and DOD does not expect to complete the related action items until fiscal year 2015. In May 2012, GAO will report on its assessment of DOD's implementation of the Plan.

Action 2 progress

DOD continues to implement its November 2010 Plan, which is, in part, focused on improving demand forecasting practices and tracking the efficiency of inventory processes. One of the Plan's nine subplans directly addresses demand forecasting weaknesses, including (1) identifying improved methods and techniques for demand forecasting, (2) identifying and implementing standard metrics to assess forecasting accuracy and bias, (3) expanding and refining a departmentwide structure for collaborative forecasting, (4) modifying approaches to setting of inventory levels for low-demand items, and (5) examining how investment risk for new consumable items can be reduced between the Defense Logistics Agency and the military departments. Efforts to address these weaknesses are scheduled to occur into fiscal year 2015; therefore, it is too early to assess DOD's progress in improving demand forecasting. Additionally, the Plan includes an action to establish departmentwide metrics to track and monitor the efficiency of DOD inventory operations; however, these efforts are ongoing and have not been finalized.

---

[33]GAO, *DOD's 2010 Comprehensive Inventory Management Improvement Plan Addressed Statutory Requirements, But Faces Implementation Challenges,* GAO-11-240R (Washington, D.C.: Jan. 7, 2011).
[34]Inventory that is not in DOD's possession but for which a contract has been awarded or funds have been obligated is considered to be on-order.

Overall assessment

Action 1

The Department of Defense (DOD) should revise guidance to specifically require the retention of life-cycle operating and support (O&S) cost estimates for major weapon systems, as well as the supporting documentation used to develop these estimates.

Partially addressed

Action 2

DOD should identify the cost elements needed to track and assess actual O&S costs for effective cost analysis and program management for major weapon systems, and require the collection of these elements in the services' O&S cost visibility data systems.

Partially addressed

Action 3

DOD should require the services to periodically update life-cycle O&S cost estimates for major weapon systems after these systems are acquired, which would enhance DOD's ability to compare actual performance to planned or expected results.

Partially addressed

Defense

40. More comprehensive and complete cost data can help DOD improve the cost-effectiveness of **sustaining weapon systems**

Action 1 progress

According to DOD officials, DOD is revising its acquisition and cost-estimating policies to include this requirement. These policies are expected to be issued in 2012.

Additionally, the National Defense Authorization Act for Fiscal Year 2012 requires the Secretary of Defense to issue guidance regarding O&S costs for major weapon systems, including requiring the military departments to retain each estimate of O&S costs that is developed at any time during the life-cycle of a major weapon system, together with supporting documentation used to develop the estimate.[35] The guidance was due not later than 180 days after the date of the enactment of the act, which was on December 31, 2011. As of February 10, 2012, the guidance had not been issued.

Action 2 progress

According to DOD officials, DOD has studied potential improvements to the services' O&S cost visibility data systems and is in the process of revising guidance.

The Secretary of Defense was also required under the above act to issue guidance to establish standard requirements for the collection of data on O&S costs for major weapon systems and require the military departments to revise their cost visibility data systems to ensure that they collect complete and accurate data and make such data available in a timely manner.[36] This guidance has not yet been issued.

Action 3 progress

According to DOD officials, DOD is revising its acquisition policy to include this requirement. The revised acquisition policy is expected to be issued in 2012.

The Secretary of Defense was also required under the act to issue guidance to require the military departments to update estimates of O&S costs periodically throughout the life-cycle of a major weapon system, to determine whether preliminary information and assumptions remain relevant and accurate, and to identify and record reasons for variances.[37] Guidance in this area has not yet been issued.

---

[35] See Pub. L. No. 112-81, § 832(a), (b)(2) (2011).

[36] See § 832(b)(4).

[37] See § 832(b)(3).

Action 4

DOD should require program offices to collect and report detailed support cost data for their performance-based logistics arrangements.

Partially addressed

Action 4 progress

DOD has been evaluating alternatives to improve contractor cost reporting. On the basis of their evaluation, DOD officials expect to make policy revisions in 2012.

Additionally, the National Defense Authorization Act for Fiscal Year 2012 requires the Secretary of Defense to issue guidance to establish standard requirements for the collection and reporting of data on O&S costs for major weapon systems by contractors performing weapon system sustainment functions in an appropriate format, and develop contract clauses to ensure that contractors comply with such requirements.[38] As noted above, guidance has not yet been issued.

Action 5

DOD should revise guidance to require the development of performance-based logistics business case analyses to better support the decision-making process on the use of these arrangements.

Partially addressed

Action 5 progress

According to DOD officials, DOD is in the process of revising its acquisition policy to include this requirement. Further, an interim directive, valid through December 2012, was issued that requires the periodic revalidation of business case analyses for major defense acquisition programs and major weapon system programs. However, DOD has not yet formally revised its acquisition policy.

Action 6

DOD should define the elements to be included in these performance-based logistics business case analyses so they are comprehensive and sound.

Addressed

Action 6 progress

In April 2011, DOD issued a Product Support Business Case Analysis Guidebook that provides additional details regarding the elements of a business case analysis. The updated guidebook also indicates that program offices will revalidate the previous product support strategy business case analysis every 5 years or prior to a change in the weapon system's product support strategy, as required of product support managers by a provision in the National Defense Authorization Act for Fiscal Year 2010.[39]

For more information, contact Cary B. Russell at (404) 679-1808 or russellc@gao.gov.

See GAO-11-318SP Actions Needed

---

[38] See § 832(b)(5).
[39] See Pub. L. No. 111-84, § 805(b)(2)(F) (2009).

Overall assessment

Action 1

If the Corrosion Office wishes to convince the Department of Defense (DOD) and congressional decision makers that more fully funding its corrosion prevention programs could provide significant return on investment, the Corrosion Office needs to complete the validation of return on investment estimates in order to demonstrate the costs and benefits of its corrosion prevention and control projects.

Partially addressed

Defense

41. Improved **corrosion prevention** and control practices could help DOD avoid billions in unnecessary costs over time

Action 1 progress

According to DOD officials, DOD has begun to validate the return on investments on corrosion projects that have been completed to demonstrate the costs and benefits of the projects. DOD's *Corrosion Prevention and Mitigation Strategic Plan* suggests that for corrosion projects that have completed research and development, transitioned to service use, and been in use for 2 years, a project review will be done to validate the overall impact and return on investment.[40] According to DOD officials, the department has completed validating returns on investment on 33 out of 112 projects that were identified in fiscal years 2005 through 2008. However, DOD needs to effectively implement the ongoing process to validate projects' return on investments. According to DOD officials, the department plans to validate all the completed projects.

For more information, contact Zina Merritt at (202) 512-4300 or merrittz@gao.gov.

See GAO-11-318SP Actions Needed

[40]Department of Defense, *Corrosion Policy and Oversight Office, Corrosion Prevention and Mitigation Strategic Plan*, (February 2011).

Overall assessment

Action 1

Congress may wish to consider updating eligibility criteria and targeting service, including terminating service at airports that are less remote from medium- or large-hub airports as well as changing other program criteria to consolidate subsidized air service.

Addressed ●

Action 2

Congress may wish to consider revising the program's operating requirements for providing air service to communities to improve efficiency and to better match capacity with community use.

Partially addressed

Action 3

Congress may wish to consider assessing multimodal solutions, such as more cost-effective bus service to hub airports or air taxi service, to provide communities alternatives to Essential Air Service.

Not addressed ○

Economic Development

42. Revising the **Essential Air Service** program could improve efficiency

Action 1 progress

As of February 6, 2012, the House and Senate had adopted a conference report on the FAA Modernization and Reform Act of 2012, but the legislation had not been signed by the President at the time our work was completed on February 10, 2012.

The conference report updates eligibility criteria and limits program eligibility, including the following changes:

- Only locations that have at least 10 enplanements per day during the most recent fiscal year beginning after September 30, 2012, except for locations beyond 175 miles of a large- or medium-hub airport, are considered eligible under the Essential Air Service (EAS) program, but the Secretary of Transportation is allowed to restore eligibility if certain conditions are met. Alaska and Hawaii are exempted from this change.

- For communities in the 48 contiguous United States, eligibility is limited to communities that, at any time between September 30, 2010 and September 30, 2011 (1) received Essential Air Service, or (2) received a 90-day notice of intent to terminate air service from an air carrier and the Secretary of Transportation required the air carrier to continue service.[41]

Action 2 progress

The Consolidated and Further Continuing Appropriations Act, 2012 eliminated the requirement that aircraft providing service under the program have a minimum 15-seat passenger capacity for fiscal year 2012.[42] However, changes to other operating requirements, such as flexibility in the number of flights provided or regionalization of air service, are possible.

Action 3 progress

No legislative action identified.

---

[41]H.R. Rep. 112-381, accompanying the FAA Modernization and Reform Act of 2012, H.R. 658, 112th Cong. (2012), as reported out on Feb. 1, 2012.
[42]Pub L. No. 112-55 (2011).

42. **Essential Air Service** (continued)

Action 4

The Department of Transportation may wish to consider assessing multimodal solutions, such as more cost-effective bus service to hub airports or air taxi service, to provide communities alternatives to Essential Air Service.

Addressed

Action 4 progress

In responding to this report, Department of Transportation officials stated that the department is prepared to consider multimodal or surface solutions should communities choose to apply to participate in the "Alternative EAS" program authorized by the Vision 100—Century of Aviation Reauthorization.

For more information, contact Gerald Dillingham at (202) 512-2834 or dillinghamg@gao.gov.

See GAO-11-318SP Actions Needed

Overall assessment

Action 1

The Federal Communications Commission (FCC) needs to undertake a broader rethinking of the vision, size, structure, and goals of the Universal Service Fund.

Partially addressed

Action 2

FCC needs to improve its management of the Universal Service Fund programs to address a number of GAO recommendations, including that FCC establish clear performance goals and measures for the programs.

Partially addressed

For more information, contact Mark Goldstein at (202) 512-2834 or goldsteinm@gao.gov.

See GAO-11-318SP Actions Needed

Economic Development

43. Improved design and management of the **universal service fund** as it expands to support broadband could help avoid cost increases for consumers

Action 1 progress

FCC has taken action to reform two of the four Universal Service Fund programs. FCC adopted an order in October 2011 to comprehensively reform and modernize the Universal Service Fund high-cost support mechanisms.[43] This was a significant step by FCC to restructure the high-cost program—the largest of the four Universal Service Fund programs. The design of the restructured program is intended to better target funding to bring broadband services to unserved areas. In June 2011, FCC adopted changes to the low-income program to detect and prevent duplicative claims from the same consumer[44] and, on January 31, 2012, adopted an order containing additional low-income program reforms.[45] According to FCC, these reforms will modernize the program and further reduce waste, fraud, and abuse by program participants. However, FCC is still considering some proposed changes to the rural health care program and has not undertaken any comprehensive reforms of the E-rate program.

Action 2 progress

FCC has taken action to address some of GAO's recommendations for the four Universal Service Fund programs. FCC adopted an order in October 2011 to comprehensively reform and modernize the Universal Service Fund high-cost support mechanisms. The order adopts some goals and performance measures for the restructured high-cost program, establishes a budget—although not a price cap—for the program, and reforms some of the accountability and oversight procedures governing the companies that participate in the program. FCC also established some goals and performance measures for the low-income program in its January 2012 order. In addition, FCC has taken action to improve internal controls over the Universal Service Fund programs, including conducting risk assessments of the E-rate and low income programs. FCC will still need to conduct performance evaluations to determine if its reforms are working and should conduct needs assessments to inform changes to and the establishment of goals and performance measures for the E-rate and rural health care programs.

---

[43]*Connect America Fund et al.*, FCC 11-161, Report and Order and Further Notice of Proposed Rulemaking (rel. Nov. 18, 2011).
[44]*Lifeline and Link Up Reform and Modernization et al.*, FCC 11-97, Report and Order, 26 FCC Rcd 9022 (rel. June 21, 2011).
[45]*Lifeline and Link Up Reform and Modernization et al.*, FCC 12-11, Report and Order and Further Notice of Proposed Rulemaking (rel. Feb. 6, 2012).

Overall assessment

44. The **Corps of Engineers** should provide Congress with project-level information on **unobligated balances**

Action 1

The U.S. Army Corps of Engineers (the Corps) should provide Congress with information on estimated project-level unobligated balances as a supplement to its budget presentation.

Partially addressed

Action 1 progress

According to the Corps, it has taken action to compile information on project-level unobligated balances and plans to include this information in its fiscal year 2013 budget presentation, which should be released in mid-February 2012.

For more information, contact Anu K. Mittal at (202) 512-3841, mittala@gao.gov or Melissa Emrey-Arras at (202) 512-6806, emreyarrasm@gao.gov.

See GAO-11-318SP Actions Needed

Overall assessment

Action 1

The Department of the Interior (Interior) should take steps to increase the diligent development of federal lands and waters leased for oil and gas exploration and production.

Partially addressed

Action 2

Congress may need to take action to authorize or encourage Interior to revise its rental fee structure in ways that are beyond what is specifically authorized to increase rental payments for nonproducing leases.

Not addressed

Action 3

Interior should complete its study examining how other oil and gas resource owners select fiscal parameters for leasing and adjusting oil and gas royalty rates and use that information to adjust, as appropriate, its royalty rates to a level that ensures the government a fair return. In doing so, it should ensure opportunities for substantive, two-way communication with program stakeholders.

Partially addressed

Energy

45. Improved management of federal **oil and gas resources** could result in approximately $1.8 billion[46] over 10 years

Action 1 progress

Nonfederal oil and gas resource owners are employing a range of policies to encourage diligent development of oil and gas leases, including increasing rental rates, offering shorter lease terms, and escalating royalty rates.[47] Interior is, to some extent, taking similar steps. Specifically, for a recent lease sale Interior increased the base rental rate from $6.25/acre to $7.00/acre in water depths of less than 200 meters and from $9.50/acre to $11/acre for leases in 200 meters or deeper. Interior estimates the additional nominal rental revenue received by the federal government over the life of leases issued from this sale is $27 million over the term of the leases.

Additionally, to encourage diligent development of federal oil and gas leases, both onshore and offshore, Interior sought authority to charge a $4.00/acre annual fee on nonproducing federal oil and gas leases in the fiscal year 2011 and 2012 budget requests, which would become effective upon congressional action. However, the fiscal year 2012 appropriations bill for Interior did not provide the department with such authority.

Action 2 progress

No legislative action identified.

Action 3 progress

In order to examine whether current U.S. royalty rates produce a fair return for the government overall, Interior contracted for a study to examine the total federal revenues that result from development of oil and gas resources on federal lands and waters. The study was completed in late 2011 and released publicly in 2012. Interior officials have not indicated how the information will affect royalty or other policies.

In addition, Interior has taken steps to examine royalty rates for onshore leases. Interior's Bureau of Land Management (BLM) has completed benefit-cost and economic impact analyses on adjusting onshore royalty rates. According to BLM, it is now in the process of finalizing a proposed rule to adjust royalty rates. The proposed rule is under review by Interior officials, after which it will go to OMB for review. BLM expects to publish the proposed rule in the Federal Register in early 2012.

---

[46]The Department of the Interior, Bureau of Land Management, updated the anticipated revenues from $1.75 billion to $1.8 billion in its fiscal year 2012 budget justification.
[47]GAO, *Oil and Gas Leasing: Interior Could Do More To Encourage Diligent Development*, GAO-09-74 (Washington, D.C.: October 3, 2008).

45. **Oil and gas resources** (continued)

Action 4	**Action 4 progress**
Depending on the results of the study, Congress may wish to provide additional guidance or take additional actions to enable Interior to change how it oversees federal lands and waters and the revenues derived from production of oil and gas there.	No legislative action identified.

Not addressed

Action 5	**Action 5 progress**
Interior should implement GAO's recommendations from prior reports addressing a variety of oil and gas measurement factors.	GAO has documented that Interior has taken action to implement 5 of the 19 recommendations GAO made in its March 2010 report to improve oversight of oil and gas measurement and improve confidence that the federal government is receiving its fair share of oil and gas produced from federal lands.[48] However, 14 recommendations remain open.

Partially addressed

For more information, contact Frank Rusco at (202) 512-3841 or ruscof@gao.gov.

See GAO-11-318SP Actions Needed

---

[48]GAO, *Oil and Gas Management: Interior's Oil and Gas Production Verification Efforts Do Not Provide Reasonable Assurance of Accurate Measurement of Production Volumes*, GAO-10-313 (Washington, D.C.: Mar. 15, 2010).

Overall assessment

Action 1

Until the federal government has implemented effective processes to determine the full extent to which improper payments occur and to reasonably assure that appropriate actions are taken across entities and programs to effectively recover and reduce improper payments, the federal government will not have reasonable assurance that the use of taxpayer funds is adequately safeguarded.

Partially addressed

Action 2

The level of importance the agencies and the administration place on the efforts to implement the requirements established by the Improper Payments Elimination and Recovery Act of 2010 (IPERA); Executive Order 13520, *Reducing Improper Payments*; and other guidance will be a key factor in determining their overall effectiveness in reducing improper payments and ensuring that federal funds are used efficiently and for their intended purposes.

Partially addressed

General Government

46. Efforts to address **governmentwide improper payments** could result in significant cost savings

Action 1 progress

Federal entities reported estimates of improper payment amounts that totaled $115.3 billion in fiscal year 2011, a decrease from the prior year revised estimate of $120.6 billion. Included were improper payment estimates for nine additional programs in fiscal year 2011 that did not report an estimate in fiscal year 2010, with the Department of Health and Human Services (HHS) Medicare Part D program having the highest estimate of the additional reporting programs. Nevertheless, the federal government continues to face challenges in determining the full extent of improper payments. For example, another three programs providing estimates for the first time were not included in the governmentwide totals because those programs were still developing their estimating methodologies. Also, three federal entities did not report fiscal year 2011 estimated improper payment amounts for four risk-susceptible programs, including HHS's Children's Health Insurance Program and Temporary Assistance for Needy Families. Audits of federal agencies also continue to identify internal control deficiencies over financial reporting, such as financial system limitations and information system control weaknesses, which significantly increase the risk that improper payments may occur and then may not be detected promptly.

Action 2 progress

In April 2011, the Office of Management and Budget (OMB) issued guidance on agency implementation of IPERA requirements for, among other things, reporting recovery auditing results, which are conducted to identify and reclaim overpayments. Accordingly, agencies reported recoveries of contractor and vendor overpayments of $1.2 billion during fiscal year 2011. Implementation of IPERA requirements is a step in the right direction toward providing additional transparency and helping to improve oversight and accountability, but continued agency top management attention is needed to further reduce the federal government's vulnerability to improper payments. Under OMB implementation guidance for Executive Order 13520, fiscal year 2011 was the first year that agencies were required to identify and report their improper payments in three distinct error categories. This additional information should be useful in identifying the causes of improper payments and developing corrective actions, and could assist in OMB's plans to enhance agencies' deployment of forensic technologies to help prevent fraud and error.

Additionally, the Senate Committee on Appropriations increased oversight of Department of Veterans Affairs' improper payments by directing the department to report to the Committees on Appropriations of both chambers of Congress on what steps have been taken to adopt recovery audits as a means of reducing and recovering improper payments.[49]

For more information, contact Susan Ragland at (202) 512-9500 or raglands@gao.gov.

See GAO-11-318SP Actions Needed

---

[49]S. Rep. No. 112-29 (2011).

Overall assessment

General Government

47. Promoting **competition for** the over $500 billion in **federal contracts** could potentially save billions of dollars over time

Action 1 progress

OMB has made progress in promoting competition, but needs to continue this effort. Specifically, OMB has called for agencies to reduce obligations under new, high-risk contract actions, including contracts awarded noncompetitively, by 10 percent in fiscal year 2010, but the extent to which agencies met this goal is unclear. In November 2011, GAO made a number of recommendations, including that OMB continue to focus on its savings initiative and clarify how it aligns with other new initiatives, clarify guidance on how agencies' initiatives are defined and reported, and expand the initiative to include all high-risk actions.[50] GAO also recommended that OMB report on the results of the initiative through fiscal year 2011. The agency agreed to adopt, where appropriate, GAO's recommendations regarding methodological and data concerns.

Action 2 progress

The largest federal contracting agency, the Department of Defense (DOD), has taken some actions to promote competition, specifically focusing on maximizing competition in situations where only one offer is received in a procurement utilizing competitive procedures. An April 2011 memorandum directs that if a solicitation was advertised for less than 30 days and only one offer is received, the contracting officer shall cancel and re-solicit for an additional 30 days, unless an exception or waiver is granted. Other guidance further directs that if the solicitation was open for at least 30 days, or has been re-advertised and still only one offer is received, the contracting officer shall conduct negotiations with the offeror, unless a waiver is granted, but in no event should the negotiated price exceed the price originally offered. If this guidance is implemented effectively, DOD should realize the benefits of enhanced competition. We will continue to monitor progress in promoting competition by DOD and by civilian agencies as well.

For more information, contact John P. Hutton at (202) 512-4841 or huttonj@gao.gov.

See GAO-11-318SP Actions Needed

---

[50]GAO, *Federal Contracting: OMB's Acquisition Savings Initiative Had Results, but Improvements Needed*, GAO-12-57 (Washington, D.C.: Nov. 15, 2011).

Overall assessment

Action 1

Acquisition leaders across the government need to more fully embrace the strategic sourcing initiative, beginning with collecting, maintaining, and analyzing data on current procurement spending. Then, agencies have to conduct assessments of acquisition and supply chain functions to initiate enterprisewide transformations.

Partially addressed

For more information, contact Cristina Chaplain at (202) 512-4841 or chaplainc@gao.gov.

See GAO-11-318SP Actions Needed

General Government

48. Applying **strategic sourcing** best practices throughout the federal procurement system could save billions of dollars annually

Action 1 progress

Federal agencies made progress using strategic sourcing approaches to achieve cost savings and other efficiencies, but some agencies, such as the Department of Defense (DOD), have not fully collected information on the use of strategic sourcing. In November 2011, GAO reported that almost all of the 24 largest federal agencies reported some savings in fiscal year 2010 associated with the use of strategic sourcing.[51] For example, after conducting a spend analysis of its air ambulatory services, the Bureau of Prisons reported savings of 30 percent, or about $1.5 million, from negotiating a nationwide agreement rather than relying on locally competed contracts. The Department of Homeland Security (DHS) established a departmentwide strategic sourcing program office, which reported saving about $347 million in fiscal year 2010 through a portfolio of more than 300 departmentwide contracts and by participating in the General Service Administration's Federal Strategic Sourcing Initiative. The office reported that DHS components leveraged their buying power to save more than $60 million by using volume software license agreements, $1.3 million on purchases of body armor, and about $2.8 million on office supplies. Several governmentwide federal strategic sourcing initiatives are in place and, according to officials from the Office of Management and Budget (OMB), have produced savings in areas such as domestic delivery services and wireless telecommunications. For example, OMB officials estimated the savings for fiscal year 2011 from governmentwide Federal Strategic Sourcing Initiatives for domestic delivery services to be approximately $31 million, and approximately $5.3 million on wireless telecommunications expense management services. GAO has not independently verified these estimates. In addition, GAO reported in December 2011 that one of these initiatives for office supplies produced an estimated savings of $16 million from June 2010 through August 2011.[52] However, further efforts are needed to more fully embrace strategic sourcing initiatives. For example, DOD, the government's largest purchaser, has not fully collected and assessed cost savings and other information from strategic sourcing initiatives.

[51]GAO, *Federal Contracting: OMB's Acquisition Savings Initiative Had Results, but Improvements Needed*, GAO-12-57 (Washington D.C.: Nov. 15, 2011).
[52]GAO, *Strategic Sourcing: Office Supplies Study Had Limitations, but New Initiative Shows Potential for Savings*, GAO-12-178 (Washington D.C.: Dec. 20, 2011).

Overall assessment

Action 1

Sustained progress in the use of award fees will require that contracting agencies adhere to the recent changes to the Federal Acquisition Regulation, which in 2009 prohibited the practices of rollover of unearned award fees and awarding fees to contractors that have performed unsatisfactorily.[53] Further efforts are needed by agencies to identify methods to evaluate the effectiveness of award fees as a tool for improving contractor performance.

Partially addressed

General Government

49. Adherence to new guidance on **award fee contracts** could improve agencies' use of award fees and produce savings

Action 1 progress

The five contracting agencies GAO reviewed in 2009 are working to develop and refine ways to implement and manage the use of award fees in accordance with the Federal Acquisition Regulation; however, it is too soon to determine the full impact of these actions. From August 2009 to February 2011, the National Aeronautics and Space Administration and the Departments of Defense, Energy, Homeland Security, and Health and Human Services, which comprised more than 95 percent of spending using award fees in 2008, took action by issuing policy guidance or updating agency regulation or guidance to be more consistent with the Federal Acquisition Regulation or in response to GAO's recommendations. These actions were aimed at improving award fee contracting, such as ensuring that all award fee plans include criteria related to cost, schedule, and performance and that award fees are only earned for successful outcomes. Improving agency guidance, while an important step, will need to be consistently implemented over time to achieve the desired effect of motivating excellent contractor performance. GAO will be evaluating the agencies' implementation of this action.

For more information, contact John P. Hutton at (202) 512-4841 or huttonj@gao.gov.

See GAO-11-318SP Actions Needed

[53]Rollover of unearned award fee is where unearned award fees are transferred from one evaluation period to a subsequent period, thus allowing contractors additional opportunities to earn previously unearned fees.

Overall assessment

Action 1

The Office of Management and Budget (OMB) could assist agencies in meeting a June 2010 Presidential Memorandum target of $3 billion in savings related to property disposals and other methods by developing an action plan to address key problems associated with disposing of unneeded real property, including reducing the effect of competing stakeholder interests on real property decisions.

Partially addressed

General Government

50. Agencies aim to save at least $3 billion by continued disposal of unneeded **federal real property**

Action 1 progress

OMB did not develop the recommended action plan. However, OMB is coordinating with federal agencies to finalize the governmentwide cost savings plans that it projects will exceed the $3 billion target by half a billion dollars, according to OMB officials. Further, OMB officials reported that as of the end of 2011, agencies have achieved in total $1.5 billion dollars of the $3 billion goal. GAO has not independently verified these estimates. In addition, the Civilian Real Property Realignment Act (CPRA), included in the President's fiscal year 2012 budget proposal, would streamline the real property disposal process by establishing an independent board to assist agencies in identifying unneeded real property. The proposed independent board partially responds to the challenges GAO has identified. It could address stakeholder influences by recommending federal properties for disposal or consolidation after receiving recommendations from civilian landholding agencies and independently reviewing the agencies' recommendations. CPRA would also establish an Asset Proceeds and Space Management Fund that could be used to reimburse agencies for necessary disposal costs.

A version of CPRA similar to the President's proposal was introduced in the House on May 4, 2011.[54] The bill was reported out of the House Transportation and Infrastructure Committee and passed the House of Representatives on February 7, 2012. In the Senate, CPRA was introduced on August 2, 2011.[55]

For more information, contact David Wise at (202) 512-2834 or wised@gao.gov.

See GAO-11-318SP Actions Needed

---

[54]H.R. 1734, 112th Cong. (2011).
[55]S. 1503, 112th Cong. (2011).

Overall assessment

Action 1

The Office of Management and Budget (OMB) should develop a strategy to reduce agencies' reliance on costly leasing where ownership would result in long-term savings. Such a strategy could identify the conditions under which leasing is an acceptable alternative, include an analysis of real property budget scoring issues, and provide an assessment of viable alternatives.

Partially addressed

General Government

51. Improved cost analyses used for making **federal facility ownership** and **leasing** decisions could save millions of dollars

Action 1 progress

OMB has not directly addressed leasing issues by developing the recommended strategy. OMB, however, indicated that lease savings will account for some of the targeted $3 billion savings from property disposals and other methods. The Civilian Real Property Realignment Act (CPRA), included in the President's fiscal year 2012 budget proposal, did not explicitly address the government's overreliance on leasing, but could help do so by facilitating consolidated operations where appropriate.

A similar legislative version of CPRA was introduced on May 4, 2011, which stated that one of the purposes of the act was to "reduce the reliance on costly leased space."[56] The bill was reported out of the House Transportation and Infrastructure Committee and passed the House of Representatives on February 7, 2012. In the Senate, CPRA was introduced on August 2, 2011, and also stated that one of its purposes was to "reduce the reliance on costly leased space."[57]

For more information, contact David Wise at (202) 512-2834 or wised@gao.gov.

See GAO-11-318SP Actions Needed

[56] H.R. 1734, 112th Cong. (2011).
[57] S. 1503, 112th Cong. (2011).

Overall assessment

Action 1

Office of Management and Budget (OMB) should complete planned improvements to its IT Dashboard, as well as implementation of GAO's recommendations.

Partially addressed

Action 2

Additional opportunities for potential cost savings exist with the continued use of the Dashboard by congressional committees to support critical oversight efforts.

Addressed ●

For more information, contact David A. Powner at (202) 512-9286 or pownerd@gao.gov.

See GAO-11-318SP Actions Needed

General Government

52. The Office of Management and Budget's **IT Dashboard** reportedly has already resulted in savings and can further help identify opportunities to invest more efficiently in information technology

Action 1 progress

OMB has begun implementing its planned improvements to its IT Dashboard. For example, in September 2011, OMB officials stated that work is under way to change the Dashboard's cost and schedule ratings calculations to improve insight into current performance. Specifically, officials said that the new calculations will emphasize ongoing work and reflect only development efforts, not operations and maintenance activities. In addition, in July 2011, OMB issued guidance requiring agencies to report investment work activities in increments of 6 months or less. OMB officials stated that this revised reporting process and the updated rating calculations will be reflected in a new version of the Dashboard, which is to be publicly deployed upon release of the President's Budget for fiscal year 2013. Once fully implemented by OMB, these changes could be significant steps toward improving insight into current investment performance on the Dashboard. GAO plans to evaluate the new version of the Dashboard once it is publicly available in 2012.

Action 2 progress

In 2011, congressional committees requested that GAO further review the accuracy of the data on the IT Dashboard and inform Congress on the costs and schedule performance of IT investments to help improve congressional oversight efforts. A congressional committee also recently asked GAO to utilize the Dashboard to conduct performance trend analyses of agencies' IT investments to determine if they are improving over time, and to report to Congress on the results of the review.

Overall assessment

Action 1

If the Internal Revenue Service (IRS) were to collect more information via expanded software identification numbers on tax returns, such information could support research into how software affects electronic filing.

Addressed

Action 2

IRS needs to develop a tax return reject prevention strategy, include external stakeholders in its reject working group, develop an action plan for that group, and provide clearer descriptions of why returns are being rejected.

Addressed

Action 3

IRS should determine actions needed to require software vendors to include bar codes on printed individual income tax returns and the cost of those actions. GAO continues to believe that bar coding of printed returns has the potential to reduce processing costs, facilitate access to taxpayer information, and improve compliance.

Partially addressed

Action 4

IRS should develop an overall strategy for increasing electronic filing.

Not addressed

For more information, contact James R. White at (202) 512-9110 or whitej@gao.gov.

See GAO-11-318SP Actions Needed

General Government

53. Increasing **electronic filing** of individual income **tax returns** could reduce IRS's processing costs and increase revenues by hundreds of millions of dollars

Action 1 progress

IRS updated its publication to require all tax preparation software firms to print an identifier on paper returns created with their tax preparation software.

Action 2 progress

IRS developed a reject prevention strategy that engaged stakeholders and has helped provide clearer reject descriptions.

Action 3 progress

IRS's 2012 revenue proposals included a legislative proposal that would require all taxpayers who prepare their returns electronically but print and file them on paper to print the returns with a 2-D barcode. There has been no action on this legislative proposal.

Action 4 progress

No executive action taken. IRS updated its Advanced E-file report in December 2010, which identified options to increase electronic filing, but it has yet to define an overall strategy.

Overall assessment

Action 1

The Internal Revenue Service (IRS) should continue to increase its use of return on investment (ROI) information. This will require additional research to identify the impacts of specific programs, including the effect on voluntary compliance by taxpayers.

Not addressed ○

Action 2

Once actual ROI statistics are developed for programs, and supplemented with compliance cost information, IRS could compare

- results across programs and

- actual ROI to projected ROI to determine if anticipated results were actually achieved.

Partially addressed

Action 3

IRS should coordinate with the Department of the Treasury to provide Congress with preliminary cost estimates or descriptions of resource needs for legislative proposals in future budget justifications.

Addressed

For more information, contact James R. White at (202) 512-9110 or whitej@gao.gov.

See GAO-11-318SP Actions Needed

General Government

54. Using **return on investment** information to better target IRS enforcement could reduce the tax gap; for example, a 1 percent reduction would increase tax revenues by $3.8 billion[58]

Action 1 progress

While IRS officials have reported that ROI is one of many useful management tools, IRS has not moved to extend ROI to existing enforcement programs.

Action 2 progress

IRS has developed a preliminary means of determining actual revenue collected from enforcement initiatives proposed in the fiscal year 2009 budget justification. However, actual cost information, particularly a process for determining indirect costs, is still under development. IRS cannot make comparisons without actual ROI.

Action 3 progress

For its fiscal year 2012 budget justification, IRS worked with the Department of the Treasury to determine which legislative proposals would be included in the budget, and then IRS provided aggregate cost information for all legislative proposals formulated in time to develop a cost estimate. As a result, Congress and other stakeholders obtained preliminary cost information to use when weighing the proposals.

---

[58]The net tax gap was updated in 2012 and estimated to be $385 billion for the 2006 tax year. Thus, a 1 percent reduction would increase tax revenues by $3.8 billion.

Overall assessment

General Government

55. Better management of **tax debt collection** may resolve cases faster with lower IRS costs and increase debt collected

Action 1

The Internal Revenue Service (IRS) needs to establish objectives and performance measures for the notice phase of its collection process for individual taxpayers as well as management responsibility for reviewing the performance of the notice phase.

Partially addressed

Action 1 progress

IRS established objectives and performance measures for the notice phase—the first phase of IRS's three-phase process for resolving individuals' unpaid tax debts—in February 2011. In addition, IRS has tasked the Office of Taxpayer Correspondence with responsibility for overseeing improvements to IRS correspondence, including collection notices. Although IRS has planned for its Collection Governance Council to be responsible for an annual management review of how well the notice phase of the collection process performed, IRS has not yet completed the needed review.

Action 2

IRS needs to better document the business rules and their rationales, and periodically evaluate how well they are working.

Partially addressed

Action 2 progress

IRS better documented the business rules and their rationales by preparing notice effectiveness reports for the three highest-volume collection notices, including detailed descriptions of the notices and rationales for business rules. IRS also planned an annual evaluation of the business rules. However, IRS has not yet fully implemented the plan or completed the first annual evaluation. IRS officials expect to finalize the evaluation by April 2012.

For more information, contact Michael Brostek at (202) 512-9110 or brostekm@gao.gov.

See GAO-11-318SP Actions Needed

Overall assessment

56. Broadening IRS's authority to correct **simple tax return errors** could facilitate correct tax payments and help IRS avoid costly, burdensome audits

Action 1

Congress many want to consider granting the Internal Revenue Service (IRS) broader math error authority, with appropriate safeguards against misuse of that authority, to correct errors during tax return processing.

Not addressed O

Action 1 progress

No legislative action identified.

For more information, contact Michael Brostek or James R. White at (202) 512-9110 or brostekm@gao.gov or whitej@gao.gov.

See GAO-11-318SP Actions Needed

Overall assessment

57. Enhancing **mortgage interest information** reporting could improve tax compliance

Action 1

The Internal Revenue Service (IRS) should revise Form 1098, the Mortgage Interest Statement, to include information on the address of a property securing a mortgage, mortgage balances, and an indicator of whether the mortgage is for a current year refinancing.

Not addressed ○

Action 1 progress

IRS indicated that its research staff would study changing Form 1098 to include additional information but does not have sufficient data on the volume and magnitude of noncompliance to make any changes yet.

Action 2

IRS should require mortgage-secured property addresses to be reported on other forms to help IRS detect taxpayers who fail to pay taxes on certain forgiven mortgage debt.

Not addressed ○

Action 2 progress

IRS disagreed with this recommendation after performing a benefits and impact analysis on making the change, and said that its existing enforcement programs identify and address noncompliance. IRS officials also said that the incremental benefits of the recommendation are outweighed by the additional burden that would be imposed on third-party records. GAO maintains that adding address information would be helpful for achieving greater compliance.

For more information, contact James R. White at (202) 512-9110 or whitej@gao.gov.

See GAO-11-318SP Actions Needed

Overall assessment

Action 1

The Internal Revenue Service (IRS) could determine how much additional revenue could be gained by refocusing mortgage debt enforcement efforts by taking some relatively low-cost steps, including revising the associated forms, collecting more information from taxpayers and lenders, and using third-party data to determine whether taxpayers are correctly excluding mortgage debt from taxable income.

Partially addressed

For more information, contact James R. White at (202) 512-9110 or whitej@gao.gov.

See GAO-11-318SP Actions Needed

General Government

58. More information on the types and uses of canceled debt could help IRS limit revenue losses of **forgiven mortgage debt**

Action 1 progress

IRS agreed that third-party data would be useful in identifying whether the debt being excluded is for a principal residence, and IRS began using these data sources in the examination process.

IRS also agreed to consider modifying some, but not all, of the forms associated with forgiven mortgage debts. Some of the modifications will enable IRS to collect more information from lenders about the types of debt being forgiven. However, the IRS has not yet implemented all of these form changes.

Overall assessment

Action 1

To improve the Internal Revenue Service (IRS) examinations of the real estate tax deduction, examination guidance needs to clarify the type of evidence for verifying deductibility and to require examiners to ask taxpayers to substantiate deductions that appear to include nondeductible charges that are large, unusual, or questionable.

Not addressed

Action 2

IRS needs to develop a cost-effective means of identifying local governments with potentially large nondeductible charges on their real estate tax bills, which will support targeted efforts to improve compliance. IRS then should work with these local governments to identify charges that are nondeductible and work with the localities and other third parties to help taxpayers correctly claim the deduction by clarifying for them what they can and cannot deduct. IRS should also use the information to target examinations covering the real estate tax deduction.

Addressed

For more information, contact Michael Brostek at (202) 512-9110 or brostekm@gao.gov.

See GAO-11-318SP Actions Needed

General Government

59. Better information and outreach could help increase revenues by tens or hundreds of millions of dollars annually by addressing overstated **real estate tax deductions**

Action 1 progress

No executive action taken.

Action 2 progress

IRS took steps to develop a cost-effective means of identifying local governments with potentially large nondeductible charges on their real estate tax bills, but determined that no cost-effective means was available. As a result, IRS has not been able to use such information to perform targeted outreach to improve compliance as GAO recommended. However, to meet the spirit of GAO's recommendation, IRS in 2010 distributed guidance to local jurisdictions that provided examples of what is and is not deductible and suggested that local governments consider modifying their tax bills to alert taxpayers that certain items are not allowable as deductions on their federal income tax returns.

GAO-12-453SP Follow-up on 2011 Report

Overall assessment

General Government

60. Revisions to content and use of **Form 1098-T** could help IRS enforce higher education requirements and increase revenues

Action 1

The Internal Revenue Service (IRS) should determine the feasibility of using current information reported on Form 1098-T in its compliance computer matching systems.

Partially addressed

Action 1 progress

IRS is evaluating the feasibility of using current information reported on the Form 1098-T, which educational institutions use to report information about qualifying education expenses to taxpayers and IRS, in its compliance programs. For example, IRS has begun testing compliance initiatives that involve making better use of Form 1098-T information.

Action 2

IRS should revise Form 1098-T to improve the usefulness of information on qualifying education expenses.

Partially addressed

Action 2 progress

IRS is taking steps to address possible changes to the Form 1098-T. However, before making changes to the form, IRS plans to address issues identified with the accuracy of data on Form 1098-T through outreach efforts to educational institutions.

For more information, contact James R. White at (202) 512-9110 or whitej@gao.gov.

See GAO-11-318SP Actions Needed

Overall assessment

Action 1

The Department of the Treasury's tax gap strategy should cover sole proprietor compliance in detail while coordinating it with broader tax gap reduction efforts. Such a strategy could include a mix of numerous options.

Not addressed ◯

Action 2

The Internal Revenue Service (IRS) should use its ongoing research efforts to develop a better understanding of the nature of sole proprietor noncompliance, including sole proprietors improperly claiming business losses.

Not addressed ◯

For more information, contact James R. White at (202) 512-9110 or whitej@gao.gov.

See GAO-11-318SP Actions Needed

General Government

61. Many options could improve the tax compliance of **sole proprietors** and begin to reduce their $68 billion portion of the tax gap

Action 1 progress

No executive action taken.

Action 2 progress

IRS has made minimal progress, as much is left to be done to better understand sole proprietor noncompliance, such as the improper claiming of losses. IRS has started to collect some nongeneralizable data on certain types of claimed losses during examinations of sole proprietor tax returns. IRS also is planning a research effort on tax noncompliance that is to include sole proprietors, but that research will not start until 2015.

Overall assessment

Action 1

The Internal Revenue Service (IRS) should develop at least a partial estimate for the business nonfiler rate based on its existing inventory of cases.

Not addressed

Action 2

IRS should set a deadline for developing performance data on its business nonfiler efforts.

Not addressed

Action 3

IRS should develop a plan for evaluating its new initiative, including codes for selecting nonfiler cases to pursue.

Partially addressed

Action 4

IRS should better use income data and selection codes in verifying taxpayer statements about their filing requirements.

Addressed

Action 5

IRS should study the feasibility and cost-effectiveness of using non-IRS, private data to verify taxpayer statements.

Partially addressed

For more information, contact James R. White at (202) 512-9110 or whitej@gao.gov.

See GAO-11-318SP Actions Needed

General Government

62. IRS could find additional **businesses not filing tax returns** by using third-party data, which show such businesses have billions of dollars in sales

Action 1 progress

IRS does not plan to develop a partial estimate of the business nonfiler rate, and funding to do so using operational data would likely not be available. IRS believes its existing operational data on business nonfilers are sufficient. However, a more comprehensive estimate could give IRS information that would be useful in its strategic planning and determining what priority it should place on this type of noncompliance.

Action 2 progress

IRS has determined that it does not have the necessary data that could be used to measure its business nonfiler efforts across IRS. IRS believes that developing such data would be prohibitively costly and plans to continue to use data at the operating division level.

Action 3 progress

IRS has identified ways to monitor and evaluate its codes for selecting nonfiler cases on a regular basis, but does not yet have a formal evaluation plan to guide this effort.

Action 4 progress

IRS has disseminated training material on using selection codes to verify taxpayer statements. IRS has updated the Internal Revenue Manual on the codes' use for some collections staff.

Action 5 progress

IRS has requested additional unpublished data from GAO's analysis to help it explore the feasibility of third-party data use. In addition, IRS is seeking access to the Central Contractor Registry file, which contains self-reported revenue and employment data on businesses that register annually to be awarded federal contracts. Collecting these data is an initial step in studying the use of the data.

Overall assessment

Action 1

Congress could require S corporations to use information already available to them to calculate shareholders' basis as completely as possible and report it to shareholders and the Internal Revenue Service (IRS).

Not addressed ◯

Action 2

IRS should evaluate options for improving paid tax return preparer performance, send additional guidance on S corporation requirements such as on basis calculations and adequate wage determinations to new S corporations, and provide more guidance to shareholders and tax preparers on determining adequate shareholder compensation.

Partially addressed

For more information, contact Michael Brostek at (202) 512-9110 or brostekm@gao.gov.

See GAO-11-318SP Actions Needed

General Government

63. Congress and IRS can help **S corporations** and their shareholders be more tax compliant, potentially increasing tax revenues by hundreds of millions of dollars each year

Action 1 progress

No legislative action identified.

Action 2 progress

IRS has an ongoing project to identify potential preparer noncompliance of flow-through returns.

IRS plans to work on guidance on S corporation requirements, such as on-basis calculations, during 2013.

IRS updated its guidance to S Corporations on adequate shareholder compensation about 6 months before GAO issued its December 2009 report on noncompliance with S Corporation tax rules,[59] but has not issued more guidance since then and has no scheduled date for issuing more guidance.

---

[59]GAO, *Tax Gap: Actions Needed to Address Noncompliance with S Corporation Tax Rules*, GAO-10-195 (Washington, D.C.: Dec. 15, 2009).

GAO-12-453SP Follow-up on 2011 Report

Overall assessment

Action 1

The Internal Revenue Service (IRS) should create an agencywide strategy with goals to coordinate and plan its enforcement efforts on network tax evasion. The strategy should include (1) assessing the effectiveness of network analysis tools to ensure that resources are being devoted to those that provide the largest return on investment; (2) determining whether to increase access to IRS data or collect new data for network analysis; (3) developing network analysis tools on a specific time schedule; and (4) deciding how to manage network efforts across IRS.

Partially addressed

Action 2

IRS should ensure that its staff understand the network tools and establish formal ways for users to interact with tool programmers and analysts to ensure that the network tools are easy to use and achieve goals.

Addressed ●

For more information, contact James R. White at (202) 512-9110 or whitej@gao.gov.

See GAO-11-318SP Actions Needed

General Government

64. IRS needs an agencywide approach for addressing tax evasion among the at least 1 million **networks of businesses** and related entities

Action 1 progress

IRS has not yet created a documented, agencywide strategy to manage network noncompliance efforts; however, it has elements of the strategy. For example, it continues to focus on making iterative improvements to its network analysis tools. Although these improvements are not contained within an IRS-wide strategy, they touch on assessing effectiveness. For example, IRS has taken steps to assess its most predominantly used network analysis tool. As part of an annual survey, IRS asked users of this tool about its effectiveness and to suggest improvements. IRS also certified the tool as conforming to agency guidelines and requirements for usefulness. The agency continues to develop other data and tools to address network-related noncompliance but not on a specific time schedule. IRS also had plans to create a research center that would focus on the detection of tax schemes and other abusive transactions. IRS envisioned that the proposed center would promote collaboration across IRS, help develop and use a suite of tools for addressing abusive transactions, and centralize datasets into a cohesive data-sharing strategy. However, the program was not funded in IRS's fiscal year 2011 budget. To fulfill the recommendation, IRS would at least need to create a specific approach on managing network compliance efforts across IRS that includes time frames for network analysis tool development.

Action 2 progress

IRS completed an annual survey of staff using yK-1, a network analysis tool. Results from the survey were used to enhance staff knowledge about yK-1. For example, IRS added an index to an existing yK-1 users' manual. Agency officials also reported adding updated information to training programs for new staff using yK-1. As part of the survey process, IRS held feedback sessions between programmers and users of the tool. During these discussions, participants discussed ways to make the yK-1 tool more effective. Officials representing the Large Business and International Division, which is a user of yK-1, said they were satisfied with the way the feedback loop operated.

Overall assessment

◯

General Government

65. Opportunities exist to improve the targeting of the $6 billion **research tax credit** and reduce forgone revenue

Congress could eliminate the regular credit and add a minimum base amount (equal to 50 percent of a taxpayer's current spending) to the method for computing the alternative simplified credit (ASC).

Not addressed ◯

No legislative action identified.

The Department of the Treasury issued a report on March 25, 2011, that acknowledged problems with the "regular" method for computing the credit. Despite those problems, the Department of the Treasury's report recommended making both the regular credit and the ASC permanent so as not to "disrupt" taxpayers.

For more information, contact James R. White at (202) 512-9110 or whitej@gao.gov.

See GAO-11-318SP Actions Needed

Overall assessment

Action 1

Congress should consider offering grants in lieu of credits to Community Development Entities (CDE) if it extends the program again. If it does so, Congress should require the Department of the Treasury to gather appropriate data to assess whether and to what extent the grant program increases the amount of federal subsidy provided to low-income community businesses compared to the New Markets Tax Credit; how costs for administering the program incurred by the Community Development Financial Institutions Fund, CDEs, and investors would change; and whether the grant program otherwise affects the success of efforts to assist low-income communities. One option would be for Congress to set aside a portion of funds to be used as grants and a portion to be used as tax credit allocation authority under the current structure of the program to facilitate comparison of the two program structures.

Not addressed ○

For more information, contact Michael Brostek at (202) 512-9110 or brostekm@gao.gov.

See GAO-11-318SP Actions Needed

General Government

66. Converting the **new markets tax credit** to a grant program may increase program efficiency and significantly reduce the $3.8 billion 5-year revenue cost of the program

Action 1 progress

No legislative action identified.

Overall assessment

○

General Government

67. Limiting the tax-exempt status of certain **governmental bonds** could yield revenue

---

Action 1

Congress should consider whether facilities, including hotels and golf courses, that are privately used should be financed with tax-exempt governmental bonds.

Not addressed ○

Action 1 progress

No legislative action identified.

For more information, contact Michael Brostek at (202) 512-9110 or brostekm@gao.gov.

See GAO-11-318SP Actions Needed

Overall assessment

Action 1

Congress may want to consider requiring the Internal Revenue Service (IRS) to periodically adjust for inflation, and round appropriately, the fixed-dollar amounts of civil tax penalties to account for the decrease in real value over time and so that penalties for the same infraction are consistent over time.

Partially addressed ◐

For more information, contact Michael Brostek or James R. White at (202) 512-9110 or brostekm@gao.gov or whitej@gao.gov.

See GAO-11-318SP Actions Needed

General Government

68. Adjusting **civil tax penalties** for inflation potentially could increase revenues by tens of millions of dollars per year, not counting any revenues that may result from maintaining the penalties' deterrent effect

Action 1 progress

In October 2011, Congress enacted the United States-Korea Free Trade Agreement Implementation Act, which included a provision increasing from $100 to $500 the penalty imposed on paid tax preparers who fail to comply with earned income tax credit due diligence requirements.[60]

No legislation has been identified that would require periodic inflation adjustments for all fixed penalties.

---

[60]Pub. L. No. 112-41, § 501(a) (2011).

Overall assessment

Action 1

The Internal Revenue Service (IRS) should determine if creating an automated program to identify nonresident aliens who may have improperly filed Form 1040 instead of Form 1040NR would be a cost-effective means to improve compliance.

Addressed

General Government

69. IRS may be able to systematically identify **nonresident aliens** reporting unallowed tax deductions or credits

Action 1 progress

Using various data sources, IRS studied ways to systematically identify nonresident aliens who may have improperly filed Form 1040 instead of Form 1040NR. IRS determined that establishing an automated program to identify this type of noncompliance is not cost effective at this time.

For more information, contact Michael Brostek at (202) 512-9110 or brostekm@gao.gov.

See GAO-11-318SP Actions Needed

Overall assessment

General Government

70. Tracking **undisbursed balances** in **expired grant accounts** could facilitate the reallocation of scarce resources or the return of funding to the Treasury

Action 1

The Office of Management and Budget (OMB) should instruct all executive departments and independent agencies to track undisbursed balances in expired grant accounts and report on the resolution of this funding in their annual performance plan and Performance and Accountability Reports (PAR).

Not addressed ○

Action 1 progress

OMB issued guidance in 2010 and 2011 only to certain federal departments and entities covered by the Commerce, Justice, Science, and Related Agencies Appropriations Act. OMB's guidance directed them to track and report in their respective PARs or Agency Financial Reports on undisbursed balances in grant accounts. However, its guidance included grant accounts that were still available for disbursement and was not limited only to those grant accounts eligible for closeout, as described in GAO's 2008 report. Funds in these accounts should no longer be disbursed to grantees because the period of availability to the grantee has expired.

In 2008, GAO recommended that OMB's guidance be governmentwide, not just limited to certain agencies. Because OMB's guidance included grant accounts with funds still available for disbursement, agencies have reported balances in active grant accounts, not just those eligible for closeout. Later this year, GAO plans to issue a report on the actions OMB and agencies have taken to track undisbursed balances in grant accounts that are eligible for closeout.

For more information, contact Stanley L. Czerwinski at (202) 512-6806 or czerwinskis@gao.gov.

See GAO-11-318SP Actions Needed

Overall assessment

Health

71. Preventing billions in **Medicaid improper payments** requires sustained attention and action by CMS

Action 1

The Centers for Medicare & Medicaid Services (CMS) should issue guidance to states to implement processes that better prevent payment of improper claims for controlled substances in Medicaid.

Addressed

Action 1 progress

Between December 2010 and June 2011, CMS took a number of steps to help prevent improper payments, including payments for controlled substances. Actions included the following:

- issuing a final rule to help ensure that payments are not made to providers and pharmacies debarred or excluded from Medicaid;

- issuing guidance to states to acquire and use the Drug Enforcement Administration Controlled Substance Registration File; and

- issuing guidance to states to help them prevent making payments to dead beneficiaries.

While GAO assessed this action as addressed, improper payments are a continuing concern. This area will require continued diligence by the agency to prevent such payments.

Action 2

CMS should improve its oversight of projects developed by consultants on a contingency-fee basis, in part, by routinely requesting information on these projects and associated claims.

Not addressed ○

Action 2 progress

CMS has not yet established a means by which the agency can routinely identify states' contingency-fee projects to maximize federal Medicaid reimbursements. CMS officials told GAO that they do not have the authority to require states to regularly report this information, and they were unsuccessful in their attempt to obtain such authority from Congress in 2005. In 2008, CMS stated that it was working to develop a method to regularly determine states use of contingency-fee consultants to guide its oversight efforts, but as of 2011, the agency had not done so. In addition, in response to a congressional inquiry CMS surveyed its regional offices in 2008 to identify the extent of states' use of contingency-fee consultants for federal revenue maximization projects. CMS officials told GAO in July 2011 that no plans exist to conduct another such survey. Without a means to routinely identify states' use of contingency-fee consultants, GAO remains concerned about CMS's oversight of federal revenue maximization projects.

For more information, contact Katherine Iritani at (202) 512-7114 or iritanik@gao.gov.

See GAO-11-318SP Actions Needed

Overall assessment

Action 1

The Centers for Medicare & Medicaid Services (CMS) should

- establish uniform guidance for states that set acceptable methods for calculating non-Disproportionate Share Hospital payment amounts,

- require facility specific reporting of non-Disproportionate Share Hospital supplemental payments, and

- develop a strategy to ensure that all state supplemental payment arrangements have been reviewed by CMS.

Not addressed ⭕

For more information, contact Katherine Iritani at (202) 512-7114 or iritanik@gao.gov.

See GAO-11-318SP Actions Needed

Health

72. Federal oversight over **Medicaid supplemental payments** needs improvement, which could lead to substantial cost savings

Action 1 progress

No executive action taken. In 2011, CMS officials stated that they have not established the recommended standard guidance, that legislation would be needed to give CMS the authority to require facility specific reporting, and that they have not developed a strategy to ensure that all existing supplemental payment arrangements have been reviewed.

-

Overall assessment

Action 1

The Centers for Medicare & Medicaid Services (CMS) should require its contractors to develop thresholds for unexplained increases in billing and use them to develop automated prepayment controls.

Partially addressed

Action 1 progress

CMS took action to improve Medicare payment accuracy by introducing predictive analytics to help identify patterns of potentially improper claims, but has not begun to use predictive analytics or other methods to implement this specific recommendation. The Small Business Jobs Act of 2010 requires CMS to use predictive modeling and other analytic techniques—known as predictive analytic technologies—to identify improper claims and to prevent improper payments under the Medicare fee-for-service program.[61] CMS officials told GAO that the agency issued a contract to implement predictive modeling, and its contractors began analyzing claims before payment to identify potential fraud in June 2011. The predictive modeling system assigns risk scores to groups of claims. CMS's contractors have begun to investigate whether the highest risk-scored groups of claims are fraudulent, but it is too early to determine the full impact that this may have on reducing improper payments. However, CMS has not begun to use predictive analytics or other methods to implement this specific recommendation, which is to have automated prepayment controls based on particular thresholds related to unexplained increases in billing and has not indicated that it plans to do so.

Action 2

CMS should conduct postpayment reviews on claims submitted by home health agencies with high rates of improper billing identified through prepayment review.

Not addressed

Action 2 progress

CMS has indicated that its contractors conduct postpayment medical reviews for agencies with high rates of home health services billing, as their resources permit. However, CMS has not reported any specific efforts to routinely conduct postpayment reviews on home health agencies with high rates of improper billing identified through prepayment review.

Action 3

CMS should require that physicians receive a statement of home health services that beneficiaries received based on the physicians' certification.

Not addressed

Action 3 progress

CMS has indicated that this recommendation could be costly and difficult to implement and has not reported any efforts to implement it. However, CMS has not provided any information about cost or feasibility, or tried to implement this recommendation as a demonstration in high-fraud areas to determine its cost-effectiveness as a strategy.

Action 4

CMS should direct contractors to focus on services where recovery audit contractors (RACs) are not expected to focus their reviews, and where improper payments are known to be high, specifically home health services. Such direction could make other contractors' postpayment review activities more valuable.

Addressed

For more information, contact Kathleen King at (202) 512-7114 or kingk@gao.gov.

See GAO-11-318SP Actions Needed

Action 4 progress

Because funding for medical review by the claims administration contractors is limited, starting in April 2011, CMS required each claims administration contractor to develop plans on how they would collaborate with the RACs on medical reviews. CMS required each claims administration contractor's plan to cover the types of claims best reviewed by the claims administration contractor versus the RAC, issues that the RACs could potentially review or known improper payment vulnerabilities that the RAC could help address, and providers that could be referred to the RACs for review. CMS also required and has received regular reporting on the results of this collaboration. The claims administration contractors are now reporting to CMS when they have referred to the RACs, or plan to refer as appropriate, specific issues or providers of certain services whose claims warrant further review to identify improper payments.

---

[61]Pub. L. No. 111-240 (2010).

Overall assessment

74. Potential savings in **Medicare's payment** for **health care**

Action 1

The Centers for Medicare & Medicaid Services (CMS) should develop a profiling system to identify individual physicians with inefficient practice patterns and use the results to improve the efficiency of care financed by Medicare.

Partially addressed

Action 1 progress

CMS continues its phased implementation of the Medicare Physician Feedback Program, which it developed to, among other things, identify physicians with inefficient practice patterns and help those physicians reduce their service costs. CMS established the program in 2008 and is distributing feedback reports to an increasing number of physicians. These reports can help control costs in several ways, such as providing information to physicians on how their resource use compares to their peers' and helping them develop strategies for reducing costs in their practices. In September 2011, CMS provided reports to 35 physician groups and plans to provide reports to over 20,000 individual physicians in early 2012 and to over 100,000 physicians later in 2012. CMS plans to do further testing of the reports with the goal of providing feedback reports to all applicable physicians by 2017. However, in previous testing of the reports, CMS found that physicians did not generally access those reports.

Action 2

CMS would likely have to seek legislative changes to maximize the usefulness of a physician profiling system—for example, changes that would allow CMS to incentivize beneficiaries to select efficient providers.

Not addressed

Action 2 progress

CMS has not sought such legislative changes, but it is planning to publicly report measures of physician quality and patient experience on its Web site beginning January 1, 2013. The law[62] provides for confidential reporting of measures of resource use to physicians. Consequently, these measures, which are used in combination with quality measures to determine efficiency, will not be publicly reported.

Action 3

CMS should examine the feasibility of addressing rapid growth in Medicare spending on imaging services by expanding payment safeguard mechanisms such as prior authorization for imaging services.

Not addressed

Action 3 progress

CMS has not implemented safeguards such as prior authorization.

However, CMS has taken steps to discourage excess utilization by expanding its use of the multiple procedure payment reduction for imaging services when a physician furnishes two or more services to a patient in the same session on the same day. It had previously applied the multiple procedure payment reduction to the technical component of certain imaging services. In 2012, CMS also applied the reduction to the professional component of the same services.

Action 4

Congress could consider reducing Medicare home oxygen payment rates to align them more closely with the costs of supplying home oxygen.

Not addressed

Action 4 progress

Congress did not restructure home oxygen payment rates. However, under existing provisions of law, competitive bidding for home oxygen was extended to 91 additional geographic areas. The rates from competitive bidding will likely be lower than rates currently paid by Medicare in those areas. Competitive bidding is currently underway and the resulting contracts and payment rates are scheduled to take effpect July 1, 2013.

---

[62]Pub. L. No. 111-148 (2010); Pub. L. No. 110-275 (2008).

74. Medicare's payment for health care (continued)

Action 5

CMS should address the issue of paying for overlapping services that are furnished together by systematically reviewing such services and implementing a multiple procedure payment reduction (MPPR) to capture efficiencies, where appropriate, by reducing payments to reflect the efficiencies. CMS should focus on those services that have the greatest impact on Medicare spending.

Partially addressed

Action 5 progress

In its 2012 Final Rule with Comment covering Payment Policies Under the Physician Fee Schedule and Other Revisions to Part B for CY 2012, CMS reported its analysis of advanced imaging services. For 2012, CMS is adopting an MPPR that applies a 25 percent reduction to the professional (physician's work) component of certain advanced imaging services furnished together. However, a budget neutrality provision applies. Therefore, these "savings" are redistributed to increase payments for other services and do not accrue to the Medicare program. The budget neutrality provision is law; therefore, Congress would have to remove that provision as it applies to the MPPR as it has done in certain specified cases so that savings accrue to the program.

Action 6

CMS should expand the scope of its MPPR for services furnished together by applying it to nonsurgical and nonimaging services and applying the MPPR to the part of the payment that covers a physician's work.

Not addressed

Action 6 progress

CMS has not taken executive action to expand the scope of the MPPR to nonsurgical and nonimaging services. However, in its 2012 physician fee schedule proposed rule, CMS asked for comment on two proposals for expanding the MPPR in the future: applying the MPPR to the technical portion of the payment for all imaging procedures; and applying the MPPR to the physician work portion of the payment for all imaging services as well as applying it to the technical portion of the payment to all diagnostic tests, such as cardiology and audiology. CMS may propose changes in future rulemaking.

Action 7

Congress could exempt from the budget neutrality requirement savings attributable to policies that reflect efficiencies occurring when services are furnished together.

Partially addressed

Action 7 progress

Congress has exempted certain imaging services from the budget neutrality provision. However, other imaging services remain subject to budget neutrality; "savings" from these services are redistributed to other services and do not accrue to the Medicare program.

For more information, contact James Cosgrove at (202) 512-7029 or cosgrovej@gao.gov.

See GAO-11-318SP Actions Needed

Overall assessment

Homeland Security / Law Enforcement

75. **DHS's management of acquisitions** could be strengthened to reduce cost overruns and schedule and performance shortfalls

Action 1 progress

DHS has developed plans to address management of acquisitions, including ensuring that requirements and cost estimates are well defined, and has begun to take actions to implement those plans. Specifically, to strengthen its overall acquisition management efforts, DHS reported that it planned to implement an integrated investment life cycle model (IILCM) to establish a decision-making process for investments' life cycles and that, as of December 2011, the department had chosen three portfolios to pilot this process. Further, in December 2011, DHS reported that it plans to examine lessons learned from the pilot and develop, among other things, an IILCM schedule and risk management plan, while conducting executive steering committee meetings over the next 6 months with a goal of beginning IILCM operations in the fourth quarter of 2012.

As part of this model and its other planned acquisition management reforms, DHS reported that it increased its staff during fiscal year 2011 for developing and validating life cycle cost estimates and began to develop independent cost estimates to strengthen the accuracy and credibility of program costs. To date, DHS has completed 4 validated cost estimates and is currently working to complete others. In December 2011, DHS reported that it developed a cost estimating Center of Excellence to assist components in developing reliable cost estimates and has set goals to complete baseline cost estimates for every major program and validate life-cycle cost estimates for 75 percent, or 34, of the Level 1 programs.[63] DHS also reported that the percentage of major programs with a validated cost estimate will be a key measure of its progress toward achieving these goals.

DHS also plans to establish various oversight structures and processes, such as a capabilities and requirements council to validate investment strategies and approve analyses of alternatives and operational requirements documents up front. DHS reported in June 2011 that the department planned to form the capabilities and requirements council early in the fourth quarter of 2011. However, as of December 2011, the council has not yet met.

These actions are positive steps that should help strengthen DHS's acquisition management processes to improve the department's ability to deliver major acquisition programs that meet critical mission needs on time and within budget. However, as GAO reported in July 2011, DHS is in the early stages of implementing these actions, thus it is too soon to assess their impact on reducing acquisition cost overruns and schedule and performance shortfalls at this time.[64]

---

[63]Major programs consist of Level 1 and Level 2 acquisitions. Level 1 acquisitions have life-cycle costs of $1 billion dollars or more. Level 2 acquisitions have life-cycle costs of $300 million or more, but less than $1 billion. In 2011, DHS identified 82 major acquisition programs, 45 of which were Level 1.

[64]GAO, *Homeland Security: DHS Could Strengthen Acquisitions and Development of New Technologies*, GAO-11-829T, (Washington, D.C.; July 15, 2011).

Action 2

DHS should establish and measure performance against department-approved baselines and indicators for major acquisition programs.

Partially addressed

Action 2 progress

As part of its IILCM, DHS is developing a decision support tool to track programs' cost, schedule, and performance indicators. DHS reported in December 2011 that it planned to develop training and a communications plan for institutionalizing the decision support tool and fully implement the tool by the fourth quarter of 2012. According to DHS, this tool is intended to monitor acquisition activities for all of its programs.

Action 3

DHS should ensure that its investment decisions are transparent and documented; budget decisions are informed by the results of acquisition reviews, including acquisition information and cost estimates; sufficient management resources are identified and aligned, such as acquisition staff, to implement oversight reviews in a timely manner; and acquisition program requirements are reviewed and validated.

Partially addressed

Action 3 progress

Among other things, DHS reported in December 2011, that it plans to have its Investment Review Board, once established, meet regularly to approve major program initiation decisions and assign programs to appropriate executive steering committees, which are to provide better governance to the department's highest-risk programs. DHS also reported in December 2011 that it plans to establish a program review board to allocate funds to prioritized programs and set implementation goals and timelines.

DHS reported in June 2011 that it conducted a survey of its major acquisition programs and acquisition oversight offices to identify gaps in its acquisition workforce. In addition, DHS reported in June 2011 that its first cohort of 10 contracting professionals graduated in February 2011 from a 3-year development program it established to recruit individuals into acquisition career fields, such as program management and cost estimating. In December 2011, DHS reported that 14 additional staff graduated from this program. Further, as of December 2011, DHS reported that it is developing a procurement staffing model and has completed 90 percent of the model. DHS plans to complete the model by the end of the second quarter of fiscal year 2012.

For more information, contact David C. Maurer at (202) 512-9627 or maurerd@gao.gov.

See GAO-11-318SP Actions Needed

Overall assessment

Action 1

The Department of Homeland Security (DHS) could take further actions to improve its management of research and development (R&D) efforts and reduce costs in procuring and deploying programs that have not been fully tested, including rigorously testing devices using actual agency operational tactics before making decisions on acquisitions.

Partially addressed

Homeland Security / Law Enforcement

76. Improvements in **managing research and development** could help reduce inefficiencies and costs for homeland security

Action 1 progress

In June and December 2011, DHS reported that it planned to establish a new model for managing departmentwide investments across their life cycles and that the Science and Technology Directorate (S&T) has become an integral part of DHS's acquisition review process. In July 2011, GAO reported that under this plan, S&T was to be involved in each phase of the investment life cycle and participate in new councils and boards that DHS was planning to create to help ensure that test and evaluation methods are appropriately considered as part of DHS's overall R&D investment strategies.[65] GAO further reported that the new councils and boards DHS was planning to establish were to be responsible for overseeing key acquisition decisions for major programs, including ensuring that testing and evaluation (T&E) is completed. DHS plans to complete the design, testing, and roll out this new approach, including the establishment of new councils and boards, by the end of fiscal year 2012 and has taken steps to do so. For example, since its June 2011 update, DHS established a new Executive Steering Council to test this new approach for enhancing oversight.

In June 2011, GAO reported that S&T was meeting some of its T&E oversight requirements, but additional steps were needed to ensure that all requirements were met.[66] GAO also reported that S&T's T&E Council was working with component program managers to strengthen R&D and T&E processes, such as developing program requirements and ensuring the appropriate T&E is complete before implementation. In addition, GAO reported in November 2011 that S&T recently reorganized and established an office to provide operations analysis, systems engineering, test and evaluation, and standards development support to DHS component program offices.[67]

While DHS has made some progress in these areas, it will be important for the agency to follow through on the establishment of these new processes and councils.

[65]GAO, *Homeland Security: DHS Could Strengthen Acquisitions and Development of New Technologies*, GAO-11-829T (Washington, D.C.: July 15, 2011).
[66]GAO, *DHS Science and Technology: Additional Steps Needed to Ensure Test and Evaluation Requirements Are Met*, GAO-11-596 (Washington, D.C.: June 15, 2011).
[67]GAO, *DHS Research and Development: Science and Technology Directorate's Test and Evaluation and Reorganization Efforts*, GAO-12-239T (Washington, D.C.: Nov. 17, 2011).

Action 2

DHS should conduct cost-benefit analyses as part of research, development, and testing efforts, which would help DHS and congressional decision makers better assess and prioritize investment decisions, including assessing possible program alternatives that could be more cost-effective.

Partially addressed

Action 2 progress

DHS reported in December 2011 that it is working with its components to improve the quality and accuracy of cost estimates and has increased its staff during fiscal year 2011 to develop independent cost estimates, a GAO best practice, to ensure the accuracy and credibility of program costs. However, in June 2011, DHS also reported that it was unable to hire the staff needed to fully implement its plans due to lack of resources. GAO reported in June 2011 that such cost estimates are important first steps for agencies in allowing them to conduct cost-benefit analyses and analyses of alternatives.[68] To date, DHS has completed 4 validated cost estimates out of 135 major programs over the last year and is currently working to complete others. In December 2011, DHS reported that it developed a cost estimating Center of Excellence to assist components in developing reliable cost estimates and has set a goal to complete cost estimates for all major programs. DHS also reported that the percentage of major programs with a validated cost estimate will now be a key goal.

DHS also plans to establish various structures and processes to oversee program research, development, and testing, including the Capabilities and Requirements Council, which is to validate investment strategies and approve program analyses of alternatives and operational requirements documents up front. DHS reported in June 2011 that the department planned to form the Capabilities and Requirements Council early in the fourth quarter of 2011; however, as of December 2011 the council has not yet met. In addition, GAO reported in June and November 2011 that S&T reviewed and approved key T&E documents and plans for major investments as required by DHS's T&E directive, such as documents outlining a program requirements and capabilities.[69] However, GAO reported that S&T could better document its review of component acquisition documents and recommended that they develop a mechanism to do so.

While DHS has made some progress in the areas of assessing costs and program alternatives and benefits, it will be important for the agency to follow through on its new processes and councils.

For more information, contact David C. Maurer at (202) 512-9627 or maurerd@gao.gov.

See GAO-11-318SP Actions Needed

---

[68]GAO, *DOD Weapon Systems: Missed Trade-off Opportunities During Requirements Reviews*, GAO-11-502 (Washington, D.C.: June 16, 2011).
[69]GAO-11-596 and GAO-12-239T.

Overall assessment

77. Validation of **TSA's behavior-based screening** program is needed to justify funding or expansion

Action 1

The Department of Homeland Security (DHS) should use an independent panel of experts to assess the methodology of its initial validation study of the Transportation Security Administration's (TSA) behavior detection program to provide DHS with additional assurance regarding whether the study's methodology is sufficiently comprehensive to validate the Screening of Passengers by Observation Techniques (SPOT) program.

Partially addressed

Action 1 progress

In April 2011, DHS completed an initial validation study. However, this study's methodology was not sufficiently comprehensive to validate the program and determine the extent to which behavior-based screening can be used for counterterrorism purposes in the aviation environment. Instead, the study was designed to determine the extent to which SPOT was more effective than random screening at identifying security threats and how the program's behaviors correlate to identifying high-risk travelers. DHS's study made recommendations related to the need for further validation efforts, comparing SPOT with other screening programs, and broader program evaluation issues, some of which echoed previous GAO recommendations. These recommendations are intended to help the program conduct a more comprehensive validation of whether the science can be used for counterterrorism purposes in the aviation environment. Given the broad scope of the additional work and related resources identified by DHS for addressing the recommendations, it could take several years to complete. According to TSA, the program is undertaking actions to address some of DHS's recommendations, such as conducting additional analysis of the program's behaviors and associated SPOT scoring system in coordination with DHS's Science and Technology Directorate. According to TSA, a refined list of the behaviors and appearances used in the SPOT program to identify high-risk passengers will be completed by mid-2012. TSA is taking actions to refine the program, but questions related to the program's validity will remain until TSA demonstrates that using behavior detection techniques can help secure the aviation system against terrorist threats.

Action 2

DHS could conduct additional research to provide additional information on the extent to which SPOT can be effectively implemented in airports and to help determine the need for periodic refresher training.

Partially addressed

Action 2 progress

TSA completed an annual training analysis to identify gaps in its training curricula related to SPOT and as a result, was developing a training plan as of November 2011. According to TSA, this plan will identify new training courses, additional recurrent training, and required updates to the current training curricula. TSA expects to complete this plan by early 2012 and revise it annually. TSA has begun to provide refresher training to all SPOT airports and plans to complete this effort by the end of 2012.

Action 3

Congress may wish to consider limiting program funding pending receipt of an independent assessment of TSA's SPOT program. Specifically, Congress could consider freezing appropriation levels for the SPOT program at the 2010 level until the validation effort is completed.

Addressed

Action 3 progress

Program funds were frozen at fiscal year 2010 levels for fiscal year 2011. The conference report accompanying the consolidated appropriations act for fiscal year 2012 stated that funding was included for 145 additional behavior detection officers.[70] This increase is less than half of TSA's fiscal year 2012 request for 350 full-time behavior detection officers. The conference report also directed TSA to brief congressional committees no later than 90 days after the enactment of the act on its plans and actions to implement recommendations from the DHS validation study and GAO's May 2010 report.[71]

---

[70]H.R. Rep. No. 112-331, at 971 (2011) (Conf. Rep.).

[71]See GAO, *Aviation Security: Efforts to Validate TSA's Passenger Screening Behavior Detection Program Underway, but Opportunities Exist to Strengthen Validation and Address Operational Challenges*, GAO-10-763 (Washington, D.C.: May 20, 2010).

77. **TSA's behavior-based screening** program (continued)

Action 4	**Action 4 progress**

Action 4

Upon completion of the validation effort, Congress may also wish to consider the study's results—including the program's effectiveness in using behavior-based screening techniques to detect terrorists in the aviation environment—in making future funding decisions regarding the program.

Partially addressed

Action 4 progress

In July 2011, GAO reported to Congress on the initial validation study's results.[72] As noted above, fiscal year 2011 SPOT program funds were frozen at fiscal year 2010 levels. According to TSA officials, as of January 2012, TSA continues to conduct research, develop additional training, assess additional concepts of operation for the program, and develop outcome-based performance measures. However, given the broad scope of the additional work remaining to validate the science for using behavior detection techniques for counterterrorism purposes in an airport environment, additional information on these efforts could help Congress make future funding decisions regarding the SPOT program.

For more information, contact Stephen M. Lord at (202) 512-4379 or lords@gao.gov.

See GAO-11-318SP Actions Needed

[72]See GAO, *Aviation Security: TSA Has Taken Actions to Improve Security, but Additional Efforts Remain*, GAO-11-807T (Washington, D.C.: July 13, 2011).

Overall assessment

78. More efficient **baggage screening systems** could result in about $470 million in reduced TSA personnel costs over the next 5 years

Action 1

The Transportation Security Administration (TSA) might achieve savings in screening personnel costs by continuing to replace or modify older checked baggage screening systems with more efficient solutions, including in-line screening systems.

Partially addressed

Action 1 progress

In 2011, GAO reported that TSA could achieve up to $470 million in net savings based on reduced TSA staffing costs through the replacement or modification of existing checked baggage screening systems with more efficient solutions over the next 5 years. TSA agreed that the deployment of more efficient systems offers potential personnel cost savings to the federal government.

Since the issuance of GAO's 2011 report, TSA has replaced 60 stand-alone checked baggage screening machines with more efficient in-line screening systems. The Full-Year Continuing Appropriations Act, 2011, required the Secretary of Homeland Security to submit a detailed report to the Committees on Appropriations of the Senate and House of Representatives on, among other things, labor savings it achieves from the deployment of improved technologies for passengers and checked baggage screening and how those savings are being used to offset security costs or reinvested to address security vulnerabilities by August 15, 2011.[73] In January 2012, TSA stated that this report is currently under internal review and could not provide a date by which it expects to submit the labor savings to the committees.

However, as of August 2011, TSA anticipates that over the next 5 years it will support fewer projects to install more efficient systems than in the past due to TSA's shift in strategic focus from completion of optimal airport systems to replacement and upgrade of the aging explosive detection system fleet. As a result, the assumptions that GAO used to calculate projected potential savings of $470 million are now outdated. Under its new plan, however, TSA continues to deploy in-line baggage screening systems to airports with facilities capable of accommodating them, and will support projects to facilitate the installation of in-line systems if TSA determines that such systems are an optimal and cost-effective solution for a particular airport. Because TSA has changed its plan to focus on replacement of the aging fleet, it is unclear when the agency will be capable of completing the installation of more efficient solutions, including in-line screening systems, at all airports where such solutions are warranted. While TSA's plans to replace and upgrade its aging explosive detection system fleet are understandable, we believe that TSA should continue to pursue the installation of more efficient screening solutions to the extent possible.

For more information, contact Stephen M. Lord at (202) 512-4379 or lords@gao.gov.

See GAO-11-318SP Actions Needed

---

[73]Pub. L. No. 112-10, Div. B, § 1616 (2011).

Overall assessment

Action 1

Congress could clarify the purposes for which the $639.4 million in unobligated balances are available. The unobligated balances have remained in U.S. Customs and Border Protection's (CBP) Customs User Fee Account for more than 10 years.

Partially addressed ◑

For more information, contact Susan Irving at (202) 512-6806 or irvings@gao.gov.

See GAO-11-318SP Actions Needed

General Government

79. Clarifying availability of certain **customs fee collections** could produce a one-time savings of $640 million

Action 1 progress

The House Report accompanying the 2012 Department of Homeland Security Appropriations bill[74] directed the Office of the Chief Financial Officer and CBP to report on the appropriate application of these funds no later than 30 days after the date of enactment of the 2012 Appropriations Act (i.e., January 23, 2012.)

On January 27, 2012, officials from the Department of Homeland Security stated that the department is working with CBP and the Appropriations Committees to schedule a briefing on this issue.

---

[74]H.R. Rep. No. 112-91, at 27 (2011).

GAO-12-453SP Follow-up on 2011 Report

Overall assessment

Action 1

Congress could consider giving the Internal Revenue Service (IRS) the authority to collect the information that the Social Security Administration needs on government pension income to administer the Government Pension Offset and the Windfall Elimination Provision accurately and fairly.

Not addressed ◯

For more information, contact Charles A. Jeszeck at (202) 512-7036 or jeszeckC@gao.gov.

See GAO-11-318SP Actions Needed

Income Security

80. **Social Security** needs data on pensions from noncovered earnings to better enforce **offsets** and ensure benefit fairness, estimated to result in $2.4-$2.9 billion savings over 10 years

Action 1 progress

No legislative action identified.

Overall assessment

International Affairs

81. Congress could pursue several options to improve collection of **antidumping** and **countervailing duties**

Action 1

Congress could eliminate the retrospective component of the U.S. antidumping and countervailing duty system and, instead, treat the antidumping and countervailing duties assessed at the time the product enters the country as final.

Not addressed

Action 1 progress

No legislative action identified.

Action 2

Congress could choose to provide the Department of Commerce the discretion to require companies applying for a new shipper review to have a greater volume of imports before establishing an individual antidumping and countervailing duty rate.

Not addressed O

Action 2 progress

No legislative action identified.

For more information, contact Alfredo Gomez at (202) 512-4101 or gomezj@gao.gov

See GAO-11-318SP Actions Needed

Enclosure III: Scope and Methodology

In March 2011, GAO issued its first annual report to the Congress on potential duplication, overlap, and fragmentation in the federal government.[1] The report also identified opportunities to achieve cost savings and enhance revenues. We identified 81 areas—which span a wide range of government missions[2]—with a total of 176 actions[3] that the Congress and the executive branch could take to reduce or eliminate unnecessary duplication, overlap, and fragmentation or achieve other potential financial benefits. We also presented areas where programs may be able to achieve greater efficiencies or become more effective in providing government services. In many areas, we suggested actions—identifying some new options, as well as underscoring numerous existing GAO recommendations—that policymakers could consider.

To examine the extent to which the legislative and executive branches have made progress in implementing actions in the 81 areas, we reviewed relevant legislation and documents such as budgets, policies, strategic and implementation plans, guidance, and other information related to the 176 actions included in our report. We also analyzed, to the extent possible, whether or not financial or other benefits have been attained, and included this information as appropriate. In addition, we discussed the implementation status of the areas with officials at the relevant agencies.

To assess the progress of the legislative and executive branches in implementing the 176 actions, we developed and used the following scales:

---

[1]GAO, *Opportunities to Reduce Potential Duplication in Government Programs, Save Tax Dollars, and Enhance Revenue,* GAO-11-318SP (Washington, D.C.: Mar. 1, 2011). This report was issued in response to a new statutory requirement that GAO identify federal programs, agencies, offices, and initiatives, either within departments or governmentwide, which have duplicative goals or activities. Congress asked GAO to conduct this work and to report annually on our findings. See Pub. L. No. 111-139, §21, 124 Stat. 29 (2010), 31 U.S.C. § 712 Note.

[2]Agriculture, defense, economic development, energy, general government, health, homeland security, international affairs, and social services were among the government missions included in the March 2011 report.

[3]These actions were identified in the "Actions Needed" section for each respective issue area.

For legislative branch actions

- "addressed," means relevant legislation was enacted and addresses all aspects of the action needed;[4]

- "partially addressed," means a relevant bill has passed a committee, the House or Senate, or relevant legislation has been enacted, but only addressed part of the action needed; and

- "not addressed," means a bill may have been introduced, but did not pass out of a committee, or no relevant legislation has been introduced.

For executive branch actions

- "addressed," means implementation of the action needed has been completed;

- "partially addressed," means the action needed is in development, started but not yet completed;

- "not addressed," means the administration and/or agencies have made minimal or no progress toward implementing the action needed.

Using the legislation and documentation collected from agencies, GAO analysts and specialists working on defense, domestic, and international areas assessed progress for each of the 176 actions within their areas of expertise. A core group of GAO staff examined all 176 assessments to ensure consistent and systematic application of the criteria, and made adjustments as appropriate.

After GAO analysts completed their assessments of the 176 actions, we made an overall assessment for each of the 81 areas using the following scale:

- "addressed" if all actions needed in that area were addressed;

- "partially addressed" if at least one action needed in that area showed some progress toward implementation, but not all actions were addressed; and

- "not addressed" if none of the actions needed in that area were addressed.

---

[4]In situations where our action needed suggested that Congress should let a provision expire, we classified it as "addressed" if Congress permitted such expiration to happen.

Finally, GAO provided the draft to the agencies involved and the Office of Management and Budget for their comments and incorporated comments as appropriate.

To prepare this report, we conducted our work from July 2011 through February 2012 in accordance with all sections of GAO's Quality Assurance Framework that are relevant to our objectives. The framework requires that we plan and perform the engagement to meet our stated objectives and to discuss any limitations in our work. We believe that the information and data obtained, and the analysis conducted, provide a reasonable basis for any findings and conclusions in this product. The information in this report is current as of February 10, 2012 and does not reflect any actions that might have been taken after that date.